Republic.com
2.0

Republic.com
2.0

Cass R. Sunstein

PRINCETON UNIVERSITY PRESS

PRINCETON AND OXFORD

Published by Princeton University Press, 41 William Street,
Princeton, New Jersey 08540

In the United Kingdom: Princeton University Press, 6 Oxford Street,
Woodstock, Oxfordshire OX20 1TW

Second printing, and first paperback printing, 2009
Paperback ISBN: 978-0-691-14328-6

The Library of Congress has cataloged the cloth edition of this book as
follows

Sunstein, Cass R.
Republic.com 2.0 / Cass R. Sunstein.
p.   cm.
Includes bibliographical references and index.
ISBN-13: 978-0-691-13356-0 (hardcover : alk. paper)
1. Information society–Political aspects.   2. Internet–Political aspects.
3. Internet–Social aspects.   4. Political participation–
Computer network resources.   5. Democracy.   I. Title.
HM851.S8728 2007   303.48'33–dc22
2007008392

British Library Cataloging-in-Publication Data is available

This book has been composed in Primer Typeface

Printed on acid-free paper. ∞

press.princeton.edu

Printed in the United States of America

5   7   9   10   8   6

For MN

*No one can read all the news that's published every day, so
why not set up your page to show you the stories that
best represent your interests?*

—Google News

*Majority rule, just as majority rule, is as foolish as its critics
charge it with being. But it never is merely majority rule. . . .
The important consideration is that opportunity be given ideas to
speak and to become the possession of the multitude. The essential
need is the improvement of the methods and constitution of debate,
discussion and persuasion. That is the problem of the public.*

—John Dewey, *The Public and Its Problems*

*One must take men as they are, they tell us, and not as the world's
uninformed pedants or good-natured dreamers fancy
that they ought to be. But "as they are ought to read "as we
have made them. . . . In this way, the prophecy of the
supposedly clever statesmen is fulfilled.*

—Kant, *The Contest of Faculties*

CONTENTS

PREFACE

IN A DEMOCRACY, people do not live in echo chambers or information cocoons. They see and hear a wide range of topics and ideas. They do so even if they did not, and would not, choose to see and to hear those topics and those ideas in advance. These claims raise serious questions about certain uses of new technologies, above all the Internet, and about the astonishing growth in the power to choose—to screen in and to screen out.

Louis Brandeis, one of America's greatest Supreme Court justices, insisted that the greatest threat to freedom is "an inert people." To avoid inertness, a democratic public must certainly be free from censorship. But the system of free expression must do far more than avoid censorship; it must ensure that people are exposed to competing perspectives. The idea of free speech has an affirmative side. It imposes constraints on what government may do, but it requires a certain kind of culture as well. (George Orwell's *Nineteen Eighty-Four*, with its omnipresent, choice-denying Big Brother, is the most familiar vision of democracy's defeat; a more subtle vision is Aldous Huxley's *Brave New World*, with its pacified, choice-happy, formally free citizenry.) Members of a democratic public will not do well if they are unable to appreciate the views of their fellow citizens, or if they see one another as enemies or adversaries in some kind of war.

I was greatly surprised by the reception of the original edition of this book. I certainly did not expect the argument to prove so controversial—that so many people would be so outraged by the effort to ask some questions about the consequences of the rise of endless communications options. I was no less surprised that the book received such favorable public attention—that even though it seemed to go against the cultural grain, it seemed to have struck a kind of cultural chord. One reason, I suspect, is that the apparent polarization of the American electorate received widespread publicity at the same time that this book was originally published; my discussion could be taken to help explain at least some of that polarization. Some of the sharpest controversies in American politics, as well as the opposition between "red states" and "blue states," appeared to reflect some of the social dynamics explored here. But again to my surprise, the book seemed to resonate outside of America as well; its translation into numerous languages suggested that the question of fragmentation and the risk of polarization are lively topics in many nations.

In the years since the book was originally written, many people all over the world have become even more concerned about the risks of a situation in which like-minded people speak or listen mostly to one another. That concern has been fueled in part by the rise of terrorism, which becomes possible in part as a result of some of the social dynamics discussed here. But the dangers of echo chambers go well beyond terrorism. Democracy does best with what James Madison called a "yielding and accommodating spirit," and that spirit is at risk whenever people sort themselves into enclaves in which their own views and commitments are constantly reaffirmed. As we shall see, such sorting should not be identified with freedom, and much less with democratic self-government.

In some ways, this book is a substantial revision of its predecessor. Technology has been changing at an amazing pace, and so some of the earlier discussion was dated. In some places, I have tried to maintain pace with new developments; in others, I simply deleted passages that will inevitably become dated soon. The original edition was completed before the attacks of 9/11, and while some of the discussion directly engaged the question of extremism, I have added material about the wellsprings of terrorism, and about the use of communications technologies to promote violence. I have also added a new chapter on blogs, whose remarkable rise the original book did not anticipate.

Perhaps most important, the current edition gives much greater attention to objections and counterarguments. Many people took the original book to be an attack on the Internet, which was hardly my intention. I have tried to clarify the real goal, which is to object not to any particular technology or to make a prediction about its uses, but to explore some of the preconditions of democratic self-government and to show how unrestricted free choice might undermine those preconditions. And while this is not an empirical study, I have tried to incorporate new material about the actual effects of the Internet. Some of the new material raises some doubts about my main argument, and I have tried to engage those doubts here. I am happy to say that I have greatly altered the discussion of policy recommendations, deleting several that now seem to me badly ill-advised.

I have been lucky enough to have had countless discussions, sometimes in person but more often online, with people who think that the argument in *Republic.com* was fundamentally wrong. I have learned a lot from their arguments; my hope is that *Republic.com 2.0* has benefited from that learning.

Republic.com
2.0

1

The Daily Me

It is some time in the future. Technology has greatly increased people's ability to "filter" what they want to read, see, and hear. With the aid of the Internet, you are able to design your own newspapers and magazines. You can choose your own programming, with movies, game shows, sports, shopping, and news of your choice. You mix and match.

You need not come across topics and views that you have not sought out. Without any difficulty, you are able to see exactly what you want to see, no more and no less. You can easily find out what "people like you" tend to like and dislike. You avoid what they dislike. You take a close look at what they like.

Maybe you want to focus on sports all the time, and to avoid anything dealing with business or government. It is easy to do exactly that. Maybe you choose replays of your favorite tennis matches in the early evening, live baseball from New York at night, and professional football on the weekends. If you hate sports and want to learn about the Middle East in the evening from the perspective you find most congenial, you can do that too. If you care only about the United States and want to avoid international issues entirely, you can restrict yourself to material involving the United States. So too if you care only about Paris, or London, or Chicago, or Berlin, or Cape Town, or Beijing, or your hometown.

Perhaps you have no interest at all in "news." Maybe you find "news" impossibly boring. If so, you need not see it at all. Maybe you select programs and stories involving only music and weather. Or perhaps your interests are more specialized still, concentrating on opera, or Beethoven, or Bob Dylan, or modern dance, or some subset of one or more of the above. (Maybe you like early Dylan and hate late Dylan.)

If you are interested in politics, you may want to restrict yourself to certain points of view by hearing only from people with whom you agree. In designing your preferred newspaper, you choose among conservatives, moderates, liberals, vegetarians, the religious right, and socialists. You have your favorite columnists and bloggers; perhaps you want to hear from them and from no one else. Maybe you know that you have a bias, or at least a distinctive set of tastes, and you want to hear from people with that bias or that taste. If so, that is entirely feasible. Or perhaps you are interested in only a few topics. If you believe that the most serious problem is gun control, or climate change, or terrorism, or ethnic and religious tension, or the latest war, you might spend most of your time reading about that problem—if you wish from the point of view that you like best.

Of course everyone else has the same freedom that you do. Many people choose to avoid news altogether. Many people restrict themselves to their own preferred points of view—liberals watching and reading mostly or only liberals; moderates, moderates; conservatives, conservatives; neo-Nazis or terrorist sympathizers, Neo-Nazis or terrorist sympathizers. People in different states and in different countries make predictably different choices. The citizens of Utah see and hear different topics, and different ideas, from the citizens of Massachusetts. The citizens of France see and hear entirely different perspectives from the citizens of China and the United

2

States. And because it is so easy to learn about the choices of "people like you," countless people make the same choices that are made by others like them.

The resulting divisions run along many lines—of religion, ethnicity, nationality, wealth, age, political conviction, and more. People who consider themselves left-of-center make very different selections from those made by people who consider themselves right-of-center. Most whites avoid news and entertainment options designed for African Americans. Many African Americans focus largely on options specifically designed for them. So too with Hispanics. With the reduced importance of the general-interest magazine and newspaper and the flowering of individual programming design, different groups make fundamentally different choices.

The market for news, entertainment, and information has finally been perfected. Consumers are able to see exactly what they want. When the power to filter is unlimited, people can decide, in advance and with perfect accuracy, what they will and will not encounter. They can design something very much like a communications universe of their own choosing. And if they have trouble designing it, it can be designed for them, again with perfect accuracy.

Personalization and Democracy

IN MANY RESPECTS, our communications market is rapidly moving in the direction of this apparently utopian picture. As of this writing, many newspapers, including the *Wall Street Journal*, allow readers to create "personalized" electronic editions, containing exactly what they want, and excluding what they do not want.

3

If you are interested in getting help with the design of an entirely individual paper, you can consult an ever-growing number of sites, including individual.com (helpfully named!) and crayon.com (a less helpful name, but evocative in its own way). Reddit.com "learns what you like as you vote on existing links or submit your own!" Findory.com will help you to personalize not only news, but also blogs, videos, and podcasts. In its own enthusiastic words, "The more articles you click on, the more personalized Findory will look. Our Personalization Technology adapts the website to show you interesting and relevant information based on your reading habits."

If you put the words "personalized news" in any search engine, you will find vivid evidence of what is happening. Google News provides a case in point, with the appealing suggestion, "No one can read all the news that's published every day, so why not set up your page to show you the stories that best represent your interests?" And that is only the tip of the iceberg. Consider TiVo, the television recording system, which is designed to give "you the ultimate control over your TV viewing." TiVo will help you create "your personal TV lineup." It will also learn your tastes, so that it can "suggest other shows that you may want to record and watch based on your preferences." In reality, we are not so very far from complete personalization of the system of communications.

In 1995, MIT technology specialist Nicholas Negroponte prophesied the emergence of "the Daily Me"—a communications package that is personally designed, with each component fully chosen in advance.[1] Negroponte's prophecy was not nearly ambitious enough. As it turns out, you don't need to create a Daily Me. Others can create it for you. If people know a little bit about you, they can discover, and tell you, what "people like you" tend to like—and they can create a Daily Me, just for you, in a matter of seconds.

Many of us are applauding these developments, which obviously increase fun, convenience, and entertainment. But in the midst of the applause, we should insist on asking some questions. How will the increasing power of private control affect democracy? How will the Internet and the explosion of communications options alter the capacity of citizens to govern themselves? What are the social preconditions for a well-functioning system of democratic deliberation, or for individual freedom itself?

My purpose in this book is to cast some light on these questions. I do so by emphasizing the most striking power provided by emerging technologies, *the growing power of consumers to "filter" what they see*. In the process of discussing this power, I will attempt to provide a better understanding of the meaning of freedom of speech in a democratic society.

A large part of my aim is to explore what makes for a well-functioning system of free expression. Above all, I urge that in a diverse society, such a system requires far more than restraints on government censorship and respect for individual choices. For the last decades, this has been the preoccupation of American law and politics, and in fact the law and politics of many other nations as well, including, for example, Germany, France, England, Italy, Russia, and Israel. Censorship is indeed the largest threat to democracy and freedom. But an exclusive focus on government censorship produces serious blind spots. In particular, a well-functioning system of free expression must meet two distinctive requirements.

First, people should be exposed to materials that they would not have chosen in advance. Unplanned, unanticipated encounters are central to democracy itself. Such encounters often involve topics and points of view that people have not sought out and perhaps find quite irritating. They are important partly to ensure against fragmentation and extremism, which are predictable outcomes of any situation in which like-minded people speak only with themselves. I do not suggest that government should force people to see things that they wish to avoid. But I do contend that in a democracy deserving the name, lives should be structured so that people often come across views and topics that they have not specifically selected.

Second, many or most citizens should have a range of common experiences. Without shared experiences, a heterogeneous society will have a much more difficult time in addressing social problems. People may even find it hard to understand one another. Common experiences, emphatically including the common experiences made possible by the media, provide a form of social glue. A system of communications that radically diminishes the number of such experiences will create a number of problems, not least because of the increase in social fragmentation.

As preconditions for a well-functioning democracy, these requirements hold in any large country. They are especially important in a heterogeneous nation, one that faces an occasional risk of fragmentation. They have all the more importance as each nation becomes increasingly global and each citizen becomes, to a greater or lesser degree, a "citizen of the world." Consider, for example, the risks of terrorism, climate change, and avian flu. A sensible perspective on these risks, and others like them, is impossible to obtain if people sort themselves into echo chambers of their own design.

An insistence on these two requirements should not be rooted in nostalgia for some supposedly idyllic past. With respect to communications, the past was hardly idyllic. Compared to any other period in human history, we are in the midst of many extraordinary gains, not least from the standpoint of democracy itself. For us, nostalgia is not only unproductive but also senseless. Things are getting better, not worse. Nor should anything here be taken as a reason for "optimism" or "pessimism," two potential obstacles to clear thinking about new technological developments. If we must choose between them, by all means let us choose optimism.[2] But in view of the many potential gains and losses inevitably associated with massive technological change, any attitude of optimism or pessimism is far too general to be helpful. What I mean to provide is not a basis for pessimism, but a lens through which we might understand, a bit better than before, what makes a system of freedom of expression successful in the first place. That improved understanding will equip us to understand a free nation's own aspirations and thus help in evaluating continuing changes in the system of communications. It will also point the way toward a clearer understanding of the nature of citizenship and of its cultural prerequisites.

As we shall see, it is much too simple to say that any system of communications is desirable if and because it allows individuals to see and hear what they choose. Increased options are certainly good, and the rise of countless "niches" has many advantages. But unanticipated, unchosen exposures and shared experiences are important too.

Precursors and Intermediaries

Unlimited filtering may seem quite strange, perhaps even the stuff of science fiction. But in many ways, it is continuous with what has come before. Filtering is inevitable, a fact of life. It is as old as humanity itself. No one can see, hear, or read everything. In the course of any hour, let alone any day, every one of us engages in massive filtering, simply in order to make life manageable and coherent. Attention is a scarce commodity, and people manage their own attention, sometimes unconsciously and sometimes deliberately, in order to ensure that they are not overwhelmed.

With respect to the world of communications, moreover, a free society gives people a great deal of power to filter out unwanted materials. Only tyrannies force people to read or to watch. In free nations, those who read newspapers do not read the same newspaper; many people do not read any newspaper at all. Every day, people make choices among magazines based on their tastes and their point of view. Sports enthusiasts choose sports magazines, and in many nations they can choose a magazine focused on the sport of their choice—*Basketball Weekly*, say, or the *Practical Horseman*. Conservatives can read *National Review* or the *Weekly Standard*; countless magazines are available for those who like cars; *Dog Fancy* is a popular item for canine enthusiasts; people whose political views are somewhat left of center might like the *American Prospect*; there is even a magazine called *Cigar Aficionado*.

These are simply contemporary illustrations of a long-standing fact of life in democratic countries: a diversity of communications options and a range of possible choices. But the emerging situation does contain large differences, stemming above all from a dramatic increase in available options, a simultaneous increase in individual control over content, and a corresponding decrease in the power of *general-interest intermediaries*.[3] These include newspapers, magazines, and broadcasters. An appreciation of the social functions of general-interest intermediaries will play a large role in this book.

People who rely on such intermediaries have a range of chance encounters, involving shared experiences with diverse others, and also exposure to materials and topics that they did not seek out in advance. You might, for example, read the city newspaper and in the process find a range of stories that you would not have selected if you had the power to do so. Your eyes might come across a story about ethnic tensions in Germany, or crime in Los Angeles, or innovative business practices in Tokyo, or a terrorist attack in India, or a hurricane in New Orleans, and you might read those stories although you would hardly have placed them in your Daily Me. You might watch a particular television channel—perhaps you prefer channel 4—and when your favorite program ends, you might see the beginning of another show, perhaps a drama or news special that you would not have chosen in advance but that somehow catches your eye. Reading *Time* or *Newsweek*, you might come across a discussion of endangered species in Madagascar or genocide in Darfur, and this discussion might interest you, even affect your behavior, maybe even change your life, although you would not have sought it out in the first instance. A system in which individuals lack control over the particular content that they see has a great deal in common with a public street, where you might encounter not only friends, but also a heterogeneous array of people engaged in a wide array of activities (including perhaps bank presidents, political protesters, and panhandlers).

Some people believe that the mass media is dying—that the whole idea of general-interest intermediaries providing shared experiences and exposure to diverse topics and ideas for millions was a short episode in the history of human communications. As a prediction, this view seems overstated; even on the Internet, the mass media continues to have a huge role. But certainly the significance of the mass media has been falling over time. We should not forget that from the standpoint of human history, even in industrialized societies, general-interest intermediaries are relatively new, and far from inevitable. Newspapers, radio stations, and television broadcasters have particular histories with distinctive beginnings and possibly distinctive endings. In fact the twentieth century should be seen as the great era for the general-interest intermediary, which provided similar information and entertainment to millions of people.

The twenty-first century may well be altogether different on this score. Consider one small fact: in 1930, daily newspaper circulation was 1.3 per household, a rate that had fallen to less than 0.50 by 2003—even though the number of years of education, typically correlated with newspaper readership, rose sharply in that period. At the very least, the sheer volume of options and the power to customize are sharply diminishing the social role of the general-interest intermediary.

Politics, Freedom, and Filtering

In the course of the discussion, we will encounter many issues. Each will be treated in some detail, but for the sake of convenience, here is a quick catalogue:

- the large difference between pure populism, or direct democracy, and a democratic system that attempts to ensure deliberation and reflection as well as accountability;
- the intimate relationship between free-speech rights and social well-being, which such rights often serve;
- the pervasive risk that discussion among like-minded people will breed excessive confidence, extremism, contempt for others, and sometimes even violence;

- the potentially dangerous role of social cascades, including "cybercascades," in which information, whether true or false, spreads like wildfire;
- the enormous potential of the Internet and other communications technologies for promoting freedom in both poor and rich countries;
- the utterly implausible nature of the view that free speech is an "absolute";
- the ways in which information provided to any one of us is likely to benefit many of us;
- the critical difference between our role as citizens and our role as consumers;
- the inevitability of regulation of speech, indeed the inevitability of speech regulation benefiting those who most claim to be opposed to "regulation";
- the extent to which the extraordinary consumption opportunities created by the Internet might not really improve people's lives because for many goods, those opportunities merely accelerate the "consumption treadmill";
- the potentially destructive effects of intense market pressures on both culture and government.

But the unifying issue throughout will be the various problems, for a democratic society, that might be created by the power of complete filtering. One question, which I answer in the affirmative, is whether individual choices, innocuous and perfectly reasonable in themselves, might produce a large set of social difficulties. Another question, which I also answer in the affirmative, is whether it is important to maintain the equivalent of "street corners" or "commons" where people are exposed to things quite involuntarily. More particularly, I seek to defend a particular conception of democracy—a delibera-

11

tive conception—and to evaluate, in its terms, the outcome of a system with perfect power of filtering. I also mean to defend a conception of freedom associated with the deliberative conception of democracy and to oppose it to a conception that sees consumption choices by individuals as the very embodiment or soul of freedom.

My claim is emphatically not that street corners and general-interest intermediaries will or would disappear in a world of perfect filtering. To what extent the market will produce them or their equivalents is an empirical issue. Many people like surprises; many of us are curious, and our searches reflect our curiosity. Some people have a strong taste for street corners and for their equivalent on television and the Internet. Indeed, the Internet holds out immense promise for allowing people to be exposed to materials that used to be too hard to find, including new topics and new points of view. If you would like to find out about different forms of cancer and different views about possible treatments, you can do so in less than a minute. If you are interested in learning about the risks associated with different automobiles, a quick search will tell you a great deal. If you would like to know about a particular foreign country, from its customs to its politics to its weather, you can do better with the Internet than you could have done with the best of encyclopedias. (The amazing *Wikipedia*, produced by thousands of volunteers on the Internet, is itself one of the best of encyclopedias.)

Many older people are stunned to see how easy all this is. From the standpoint of those concerned with ensuring access to more opinions and more topics, the new communications technologies can be a terrific boon. But it remains true that many apparent "street corners," on the Internet in particular, are highly specialized, limited as they are to particular views. What I will argue is not that people lack curiosity or that street corners will disappear but instead that there is an insistent need for them, and that a system of freedom of expression should be viewed partly in light of that need. What I will also suggest is that there are serious dangers in a system in which individuals bypass general-interest intermediaries and restrict themselves to opinions and topics of their own choosing. In particular, I will emphasize the risks posed by any situation in which thousands or perhaps millions or even tens of millions of people are mainly listening to louder echoes of their own voices. A situation of this kind is likely to produce far worse than mere fragmentation.

What Is and What Isn't the Issue

Some clarifications, designed to narrow the issue, are now in order. I will be stressing problems on the "demand" side on the speech market. These are problems that stem not from the actions of *producers*, but instead from the choices and preferences of *consumers*. I am aware that on one view, the most important emerging problems come from large corporations, and not from the many millions, indeed billions, of individuals who make communications choices. In the long run, however, I believe that some of the most interesting questions, and certainly the most neglected ones, involve consumer behavior. This is not because consumers are usually confused, irrational, or malevolent. It is because choices that seem perfectly reasonable in isolation may, when taken together, badly disserve democratic goals.

Because of my focus on the consumers of information, I will not be discussing a wide range of issues that have engaged attention in the last decade. Many of these issues

13

involve the allegedly excessive power of large corporations or conglomerates.

- I will not deal with the feared disappearance of coverage of issues of interest to small or disadvantaged groups. That is decreasingly likely to be a problem. On the contrary, there has been a tremendous growth in "niche markets," serving groups both large and small. With a decrease in scarcity, this trend will inevitably continue. Technological development is a great ally of small groups and minorities, however defined. People with unusual or specialized tastes are not likely to be frozen out of the emerging communications universe. The opposite is much more likely to be true; they will have easy access to their preferred fare—far easier than ever before.

- I will not be exploring the fascinating increase in people's ability to participate in *creating* widely available information—through art, movies, books, science, and much more. With the Internet, any one of us might be able to make a picture, a story, or a video clip available to all of us; YouTube is merely one example. In this way, the Internet has a powerful democratizing function.[4] Countless websites are now aggregating diverse knowledge. *Wikipedia*, for example, has thousands of authors, and the very form of the wiki allows people to contribute to the creation of a product from which they simultaneously benefit. For diverse products—books, movies, cars, doctors, and much more every day—it is easy to find sources that tell you what most people think, and it is easy as well to contribute to that collective knowledge. Prediction markets, for example, aggregate the judgments of numerous forecasters, and they are proving to be remarkably accurate. There is much to be said about the growing ability of consumers to be producers too.[5] But that is not my topic here.

- I will provide little discussion of monopolistic behavior by suppliers or manipulative practices by them. That question has received considerable attention, above all in connection with the 1999—2000 antitrust litigation involving Microsoft. Undoubtedly some suppliers do try to monopolize, and some do try to manipulate; consider, for example, the fact that many browsers provide some automatic bookmarks designed to allow users to link with certain sites but not others. Every sensible producer of communications knows that a degree of filtering is a fact of life. Producers also know something equally important but less obvious: consumers' *attention* is the crucial (and scarce) commodity in the emerging market. Companies stand to gain a great deal if they can shift attention in one direction rather than another.

This is why many Internet sites provide information and entertainment to consumers for free. Consumers are actually a commodity, often "sold" to advertisers in return for money; it is therefore advertisers and not consumers who pay. This is pervasively true of radio and television.[6] To a large degree, it is true of websites too. Consider, for example, the hilarious case of Netzero.com, which provides Internet access. A few years ago, Netzero.com described itself—indeed this was its motto—as "Defender of the Free World." In an extensive advertising campaign, Netzero.com portrayed its founders as besieged witnesses before a legislative committee, defending basic liberty by protecting everyone's "right" to have access to the Internet. But is Netz-

15

ero.com really attempting to protect rights, or is it basically interested in earning profits? The truth is that Netzero.com is one of a number of for-profit companies giving inexpensive Internet access to consumers (a social benefit to be sure), but making money by promising advertisers that the consumers it services will see their commercials. There is nothing at all wrong with making money, but Netzero.com should hardly be seen as some dissident organization of altruistic patriots.

Especially in light of the overriding importance of attention, some private companies will attempt to manipulate consumers, and occasionally they will engage in monopolistic practices. Is this a problem? No unqualified answer would make sense. An important question is whether market forces will reduce the adverse effects of efforts at manipulation or monopoly. I believe that to a large extent, they will; but that is not my concern here. For a democracy, many of the most serious issues raised by the new technologies do not involve manipulation or monopolistic behavior by large companies.

- I will not be discussing private power over "code," the structure and design of programs. In an illuminating and important book, Lawrence Lessig explored the risk that private code makers will control possibilities on the Internet, in a way that compromises privacy, the free circulation of ideas, and other important social values.[7] As Lessig persuasively demonstrates, this is indeed a possible problem. But the problem should not be overstated, particularly in view of the continuing effects of extraordinary competitive forces. The movement for "open-source" software (above all Linux), in which people can contribute innovations to code, is flourishing, and in any case competitive pressures impose limits on the extent to which code makers may move in directions that consumers reject. Privacy guarantees, for example, are an emerging force on the Internet. Undoubtedly there is room, in some contexts, for a governmental role in ensuring against the abusive exercise of the private power over code. But that is not my concern here.

- In the same vein, I will put to one side the active debate over the uses of copyright law to limit the dissemination of material on the Internet and elsewhere. This is an exceedingly important debate, to be sure, but one that raises issues very different from those explored in this book.[8]
- I will not be discussing the "digital divide," at least not as this term is ordinarily understood. People concerned about this problem emphasize the existing inequality in access to new communications technologies, an inequality that divides, for example, those with and those without access to the Internet. That is indeed an important issue, certainly domestically and even more so internationally, because it threatens to aggravate existing social inequalities, many of them unjust, at the same time that it deprives many millions (perhaps billions) of people of information and opportunities. But in both the domestic and the international context, that problem seems likely to diminish over time, as new technologies, above all the Internet, are made increasingly available to people regardless of their income or wealth.[9]

Of course we should do whatever we reasonably can to accelerate the process, which will provide benefits, not least for both freedom and health, for millions and even billions. But what I will describe will operate even if everyone is on the right side of that divide, that is, even if everyone has access to the Internet. My focus, that is, will be on several other sorts of digital divides that are likely to emerge in the presence of universal access—on how reasonable choices by individual consumers might produce both individual and social harm. This point is emphatically connected with inequalities, but not in access to technologies; it does not depend in any way on inequalities there.

The digital divides that I will emphasize may or may not be a nightmare. But if I am right, there is all the reason in the world to reject the view that free markets, as embodied in the notion of "consumer sovereignty," exhaust the concerns of those who seek to evaluate any system of communications. The imagined world of innumerable, diverse editions of the Daily Me is not a utopian dream, and it would create serious problems from the democratic point of view.

2

An Analogy and an Ideal

The Neighborhood Me

THE CHANGES now being produced by new communications technologies are understated, not overstated, by the thought experiment with which I began. What is happening goes far beyond the increasingly customized computer screen.

Many of us telecommute rather than going to work; this is a growing trend. Rather than visiting the local bookstore, where we are likely to see a number of diverse people, many of us shop for books on Amazon.com. Others avoid the local stores, because one or another company is entirely delighted to deliver *Citizen Kane* and a pizza. Thus media analyst Ken Auletta enthuses, "I can sample music on my computer, then click and order. I don't have to go to a store. I don't have to get in a car. I don't have to move. God, that's heaven."[1]

If you are interested in anything at all—from computers to linens to diamonds to cars to medical advice—an online company will be happy to assist you. Indeed, if you would like to attend college, or even to get a graduate degree, you may be able to avoid the campus. College education is available online.[2]

It would be foolish to claim that this is bad, or a loss, in general or on balance. On the contrary, the dramatic increase in convenience is a wonderful blessing for consumers. Driving around in search of gifts, for example, can be a real bother. (Can you remember what this used to be like? Is it still like that for you?) For many of us, the chance to point-and-click is an extraordinary improvement. And many people, both rich and poor, take advantage of new technologies to "go" to places that they could not in any sense have visited before—South Africa, Germany, Iran, France, Venice, Beijing, stores and more stores everywhere, an immense variety of specialized doctors' offices. But it is far from foolish to worry that for millions of people, the consequence of this increased convenience is to decrease the set of chance encounters with diverse others—and also to be concerned about the consequence of the decrease for democracy and citizenship.

Or consider the concept of collaborative filtering—an intriguing feature on a number of sites, one that has now become routine and is rapidly becoming part of daily life online. Once you order a book from Amazon.com, for example, Amazon.com is in a position to tell you the choices of other people who like that particular book. Once you have ordered a number of books, Amazon.com knows, and will tell you, the other books—and music and movies—that you are likely to like, based on what people like you have liked. Other websites are prepared to tell you which new movies you'll enjoy and which you won't—simply by asking you to rate certain movies, then matching your ratings to those of other people, and then finding out what people like you think about movies that you haven't seen. (Netflix is particularly happy to help you on this count.) For music, there are many possibilities: Musicmobs and Indy are examples, with the latter proclaiming, "Indy is a music discovery program that learns what you like, and plays more of it." With wikilens, you can see

20

what people like you like in restaurants, books, and beers, as well as music and movies.

"Personalized shopping" is becoming readily available, and it is intended to match the interests and purchasing patterns of customers for a dazzling array of products, including radios, computers, fabrics, pens, room designs, and wish lists. (Put "personalized shopping" in Google, and watch what comes up.) Or consider the suggestion that before long we will "have virtual celebrities. . . . They'll look terrific. In fact, they'll look so terrific that their faces will be exactly what *you* think is beautiful and not necessarily what your neighbor thinks, because they'll be customized for each home."[3] (Is it surprising to hear that several websites provide personalized romance stories? That at least one asks you for information about "your fantasy lover," and then it designs a story to suit your tastes?)

In many ways what is happening is quite wonderful, and some of the recommendations from Amazon.com, Netflix, and analogous services are miraculously good, even uncanny. Countless people have discovered new favorite books, movies, and bands through this route. But it might well be disturbing if the consequence is to encourage people to narrow their horizons, or to cater to their existing tastes rather than to allow them to form new ones. The problem is a real one for movies and music, but it is probably most serious in the democratic domain. Suppose, for example, that people with a certain political conviction find themselves learning about more and more authors with the same view and thus strengthening their preexisting judgments, only because most of what they are encouraged to read says the same thing. In a democratic society, might this not be troubling?

The underlying issues here are best approached through two different routes. The first involves an unusual and somewhat exotic constitutional doctrine, based on the idea of the "public forum." The second involves a general constitutional ideal, indeed the most general constitutional ideal of all: that of deliberative democracy. As we will see, a decline in common experiences and a system of individualized filtering might compromise that ideal. As a corrective, we might build on the understandings that lie behind the notion that a free society creates a set of public forums, providing speakers' access to a diverse people, and ensuring in the process that each of us hears a wide range of speakers, spanning many topics and opinions.

The Idea of the Public Forum

In the common understanding, the free-speech principle is taken to forbid government from "censoring" speech of which it disapproves. In the standard cases, the government attempts to impose penalties, whether civil or criminal, on political dissent, libelous speech, commercial advertising, or sexually explicit speech. The question is whether the government has a legitimate, and sufficiently weighty, reason for restricting the speech that it seeks to control.

This is indeed what most of the law of free speech is about. In Germany, France, Russia, the United States, Mexico, and many other nations, constitutional debates focus on the limits of censorship. But in free countries, an important part of free-speech law takes a quite different form. In the United States, for example, the Supreme Court has ruled that streets and parks must be kept open to the public for expressive activity. In the leading case, from the early part of the twentieth century, the Court said, "Wherever the title of streets and parks may rest, they have immemorially been held in trust for the use of the public and time out of mind, have been used for the purposes of assembly, communicating thought between citizens, and discussing public questions. Such use of the streets and public places has, from ancient times, been a part of the privileges, immunities, rights, and liberties of citizens."[4]

Hence governments are obliged to allow speech to occur freely on public streets and in public parks—even if many citizens would prefer to have peace and quiet, and even if it seems irritating to come across protesters and dissidents when you are simply walking home or to the local grocery store. If you see protestors on a local street, and you wonder why they are allowed to be there (and perhaps to bother you), the answer is that the Constitution gives them a right to do so.

To be sure, the government is allowed to impose restrictions on the "time, place, and manner" of speech in public places. No one has a right to set off fireworks or to use loudspeakers on the public streets at 3 a.m. in order to complain about crime, global warming, or the size of the defense budget. But time, place, and manner restrictions must be both reasonable and limited. Government is essentially obliged to allow speakers, whatever their views, to use public property to convey messages of their choosing.

A distinctive feature of the public-forum doctrine is that it creates *a right of speakers' access, both to places and to people*. Another distinctive feature is that the public-forum doctrine creates a right, not to avoid governmentally imposed *penalties* on speech, but to ensure government *subsidies* of speech. There is no question that taxpayers are required to support the expressive activity that, under the public-forum doctrine, must be permitted on the streets and parks. Indeed, the costs that taxpayers devote to maintaining open streets and parks, from cleaning to maintenance, can be quite high.

Thus the public forum represents one area of law in which the right to free speech demands a public subsidy to speakers.

Just Streets and Parks? Of Airports and the Internet

As a matter of principle, there seems to be good reason to expand the public forum well beyond streets and parks. In the modern era, other places have increasingly come to occupy the role of traditional public forums. The mass media and the Internet as well have become far more important than streets and parks as arenas in which expressive activity occurs.

Nonetheless, the Supreme Court has been wary of expanding the public-forum doctrine beyond streets and parks. Perhaps the Court's wariness stems from a belief that once the historical touchstone is abandoned, lines will be extremely hard to draw, and judges will be besieged with requests for rights of access to private and public property. Thus the Court has rejected the seemingly plausible argument that many other places should be seen as public forums too. In particular, it has been urged that airports, more than streets and parks, are crucial to reaching a heterogeneous public; airports are places where diverse people congregate and where it is important to have access if you want to speak to large numbers of people. The Court was not convinced, responding that the public-forum idea should be understood by reference to historical practices. Airports certainly have not been treated as public forums from "ancient times."[5]

But at the same time, some members of the Court have shown considerable uneasiness with a purely historical test. In the most vivid passage on the point, Supreme Court Justice Anthony Kennedy wrote: "Minds are not changed in streets and parks as they once were. To an increasing degree, the more significant interchanges of ideas and shaping of public consciousness occur in mass and electronic media. The extent of public entitlement to participate in those means of communication may be changed as technologies change."[6] What Justice Kennedy is recognizing here is the serious problem of how to "translate" the public-forum idea into the modern technological environment. And if the Supreme Court is unwilling to do any such translating, it remains open for Congress, state governments, and ordinary citizens to consider doing exactly that. In other words, the Court may not be prepared to say, as a matter of constitutional law, that the public-forum idea extends beyond streets and parks. But even if the Court is unprepared to act, Congress and state governments are permitted to conclude that a free society requires a right of access to areas where many people meet.

Indeed, private and public institutions might reach such conclusions on their own, and take steps to ensure that people are exposed to a diversity of views. Airports and train stations might decide to remain open for expressive activity—as many now are. Broadcasters might attempt, on their own, to create the functional equivalent of public forums, allowing people with a wide range of views to participate—as many now do. An important question is how to carry forward the goals of old law in the modern era.

Why Public Forums? Of Access, Unplanned Encounters, and Irritations

The Supreme Court has given little sense of why, exactly, it is important to ensure that the streets and parks remain open to speakers. This is the question that must be answered if we

25

are to know whether, and how, to understand the relationship of the public-forum doctrine to contemporary problems.

We can make some progress here by noticing that the public-forum doctrine promotes three important goals.[7] *First*, it ensures that speakers can have access to a wide array of people. If you want to claim that taxes are too high, that religious diversity is not being respected, or that police brutality is widespread, you are able to press this argument on many people who might otherwise fail to hear the message. The diverse people who walk the streets and use the parks are likely to hear speakers' arguments about taxes, religious plurality, or the police; they might also learn about the nature and intensity of views held by their fellow citizens. Perhaps some people's views change because of what they learn; perhaps they will become curious, enough so to investigate the question on their own. It does not much matter if this happens a little or a lot. What is important is that speakers are allowed to press concerns that might otherwise be ignored by their fellow citizens.

On the speakers' side, the public-forum doctrine thus *creates a right of general access to heterogeneous citizens*. On the listeners' side, the public forum creates not exactly a right, but an opportunity, if perhaps an unwelcome one: *shared exposure to diverse speakers with diverse views and complaints*. It is important to emphasize that the exposure is shared. Many people will be simultaneously exposed to the same views and complaints, and they will encounter views and complaints that some of them might have refused to seek out in the first instance. Indeed, the exposure might well be considered, much of the time, irritating or worse.

Second, the public-forum doctrine allows speakers not only to have general access to heterogeneous people, but also to specific people and specific institutions with whom they have a complaint. Suppose, for example, that you believe that the state legislature has behaved irresponsibly with respect to crime or health care for children. The public forum ensures that you can make your views heard by legislators, simply by protesting in front of the state legislature itself.

The point applies to private as well as public institutions. If a clothing store is believed to have cheated customers, or to have acted in a racist manner, protestors are allowed a form of access to the store itself. This is not because they have a right to trespass on private property—no one has that right— but because a public street is highly likely to be close by, and a strategically located protest will undoubtedly catch the attention of the store and its customers. Under the public-forum doctrine, speakers are thus permitted to have access to particular audiences, and particular listeners cannot easily avoid hearing complaints that are directed against them. In other words, listeners have a sharply limited power of self-insulation. If they want to live in gated communities, they might be able to do so, but the public forum will impose a strain on their efforts.

Third, the public-forum doctrine increases the likelihood that people generally will be exposed to a wide variety of people and views. When you go to work or visit a park, it is possible that you will have a range of unexpected encounters, however fleeting or seemingly inconsequential. On your way to the office or when eating lunch in the park, you cannot easily wall yourself off from contentions or conditions that you would not have sought out in advance, or that you would avoided if you could. Here too the public-forum doctrine tends to ensure a range of experiences that are widely shared—streets and parks are public property—and also a set of exposures to diverse views and conditions. What I mean to suggest is that these exposures help promote understanding and perhaps in that sense freedom. As we will soon see, all of these points can be closely connected to democratic ideals.

We should also distinguish here between exposures that are *unplanned* and exposures that are *unwanted*. In a park, for example, you might encounter a baseball game or a group of people protesting the conduct of the police. These might be unplanned experiences; you did not choose them and you did not foresee them. But once you encounter the game or the protest, you are hardly irritated; you may even be glad to have stumbled across them. By contrast, you might also encounter homeless people or beggars asking you for money and perhaps trying to sell you something that you really don't want. If you could have "filtered out" these experiences, you would have chosen to do so. For many people, the category of unwanted—as opposed to unplanned—exposures includes a great many political activities. You might be bored by those activities and wish that they were not disturbing your stroll through the street. You might be irritated or angered by such activities, perhaps because they are disturbing your stroll, perhaps because of the content of what is being said, perhaps because of who is saying it.

It is also important to distinguish between exposures to *experiences* and exposures to *arguments*. Public forums make it more likely that people will not be able to wall themselves off from their fellow citizens. People will get a glimpse, at least, of the lives of others, as for example through encountering people from different social classes. Some of the time, however, the public-forum doctrine makes it more likely that people will have a sense, however brief, not simply of the experiences but also of the arguments being made by people with a particular point of view. You might encounter written materials, for example, that draw attention to the problem of domestic violence. The most ambitious uses of public forums are designed to alert people to arguments as well as experiences—though the latter sometimes serves as a kind of shorthand reference for the former, as when a picture or a brief encounter has the effect of thousands of words.

In referring to the goals of the public-forum doctrine, I aim to approve of encounters that are unwanted as well as unplanned, and also of exposure to experiences as well as arguments. But those who disapprove of unwanted encounters might also agree that unplanned ones are desirable, and those who believe that exposure to arguments is too demanding or too intrusive might also appreciate the value, in a heterogeneous society, of exposure to new experiences.

General-Interest Intermediaries as Unacknowledged Public Forums (of the World)

Of course there is a limit to how much can be done on streets and in parks. Even in the largest cities, streets and parks are insistently *local*. But many of the social functions of streets and parks, as public forums, are performed by other institutions too. In fact society's general-interest intermediaries— newspapers, magazines, television broadcasters—can be understood as public forums of an especially important sort.

The reasons are straightforward. When you read a city newspaper or a national magazine, your eyes will come across a number of articles that you would not have selected in advance. If you are like most people, you will read some of those articles. Perhaps you did not know that you might have an interest in the latest legislative proposal involving national security, or Social Security reform, or Somalia, or recent developments in the Middle East; but a story might catch your attention. What is true for topics is also true for points of view.

You might think that you have nothing to learn from someone whose view you abhor. But once you come across the editorial pages, you might well read what they have to say, and you might well benefit from the experience. Perhaps you will be persuaded on one point or another, or informed whether or not you are persuaded. At the same time, the front-page headline, or the cover story in a weekly magazine, is likely to have a high degree of salience for a wide range of people. While shopping at the local grocery store, you might see the cover of *Time* or *Newsweek*, and the story—about a promising politician, a new risk, a surprising development in Europe—might catch your attention, so you might pick up the issue and learn something even if you had no interest in advance.

Unplanned and unchosen encounters often turn out to do a great deal of good, for individuals and society at large. In some cases, they even change people's lives. The same is true, though in a different way, for unwanted encounters. In some cases, you might be irritated by seeing an editorial from your least favorite writer. You might wish that the editorial weren't there. But despite yourself, your curiosity might be piqued, and you might read it. Perhaps this isn't a lot of fun. But it might prompt you to reassess your own view and even to revise it. At the very least, you will have learned what many of your fellow citizens think and why they think it. What is true for arguments is also true for topics, as when you encounter, with some displeasure, a series of stories on crime or global warming or Iraq or same-sex marriage or alcohol abuse, but find yourself learning a bit, or more than a bit, from what those stories have to say.

Television broadcasters have similar functions. Maybe the best example is what has become an institution in many nations: the evening news. If you tune into the evening news, you will learn about a number of topics that you would not have chosen in advance. Because of the speed and immediacy of television, broadcasters perform these public-forum-type functions even more than general-interest intermediaries in the print media. The "lead story" on the networks is likely to have a great deal of public salience, helping to define central issues and creating a kind of shared focus of attention for many millions of people. And what happens after the lead story—the coverage of a menu of topics both domestic and international—creates something like a speakers' corner beyond anything ever imagined in Hyde Park.

None of these claims depends on a judgment that general-interest intermediaries always do an excellent—or even a good—job. Sometimes such intermediaries fail to provide even a minimal understanding of topics or opinions. Sometimes they offer a watered-down version of what most people already think. Sometimes they suffer from prejudices and biases of their own. Sometimes they deal little with substance and veer toward sound bites and sensationalism, properly deplored trends in the last decades.

What matters for present purposes is that in their best forms, general-interest intermediaries expose people to a range of topics and views at the same time that they provide shared experiences for a heterogeneous public. Indeed, general-interest intermediaries of this sort have large advantages over streets and parks precisely because most of them tend to be so much less local and so much more national, even international. Typically they expose people to questions and problems in other areas, even other nations. They even provide a form of modest, backdoor cosmopolitanism, ensuring that many people will learn something about diverse areas of the planet, regardless of whether they are much interested, initially or ever, in doing so.

Of course general-interest intermediaries are not public forums in the technical sense that the law recognizes. These are private rather than public institutions. Most important, members of the public do not have a legal right of access to them. Individual citizens are not allowed to override the editorial and economic judgments and choices of private owners. In the 1970s, a sharp constitutional debate on precisely this issue resulted in a resounding defeat for those who claimed a constitutionally guaranteed access right.[8] But the question of legal compulsion is really incidental to my central claim here. Society's general-interest intermediaries, even without legal compulsion, serve many of the functions of public forums. They promote shared experiences; they expose people to information and views that would not have been selected in advance.

Republicanism, Deliberative Democracy, and Two Kinds of Filtering

The public-forum doctrine is an odd and unusual one, especially insofar as it creates a kind of speakers' access right to people and places, subsidized by taxpayers. But the doctrine is closely associated with a longstanding constitutional ideal, one that is very far from odd: that of republican self-government.

From the beginning, the American constitutional order was designed to create a republic, as distinguished from a monarchy or a direct democracy. We cannot understand the system of freedom of expression, and the effects of new communications technologies and filtering, without reference to this ideal. It will therefore be worthwhile to spend some space on the concept of a republic, and on the way the American

Constitution understands this concept, in terms of a delibera-tive approach to democracy. And the general ideal is hardly limited to America; it plays a role in many nations committed to self-government.

In a republic, government is not managed by any king or queen; there is no sovereign operating independently of the people.[9] The American Constitution represents a firm rejec-tion of the monarchical heritage, and the framers self-con-sciously transferred sovereignty from any monarchy (with the explicit constitutional ban on "titles of nobility") to "We the People." This represents, in Gordon Wood's illuminating phrase, the "radicalism of the American revolution."[10] At the same time, the founders were extremely fearful of popular passions and prejudices, and they did not want government to translate popular desires directly into law. Indeed, they were sympathetic to a form of filtering, though one very different from what I have emphasized thus far. Rather than seeking to allow people to filter what they would see and hear, they attempted to create institutions that would "filter" popular desires so as to ensure policies that would promote the public good. Thus the structure of political representation and the system of checks and balances were designed to create a kind of filter between people and law, so as to ensure that what would emerge would be both reflective and well-informed. At the same time, the founders placed a high premium on the idea of "civic virtue," which required participants in politics to act as citizens dedicated to something other than their own self-interest, narrowly conceived.

This form of republicanism involved an attempt to create a "deliberative democracy." In this system, representatives would be accountable to the public at large. But there was also supposed to be a large degree of reflection and debate, both within the citizenry and within government itself.[11] The aspiration to deliberative democracy can be seen in many places in the constitutional design. The system of bicameralism, for example, was intended as a check on insufficiently deliberative action from one or another legislative chamber; the Senate in particular was supposed to have a "cooling" effect on popular passions. The long length of service for senators was designed to make deliberation more likely; so too for large election districts, which would reduce the power of small groups over the decisions of representatives. The Electoral College was originally a deliberative body, ensuring that the choice of the president would result from some combination of popular will and reflection and exchange on the part of representatives. Most generally, the system of checks and balances had, as its central purpose, the creation of a mechanism for promoting deliberation within the government as a whole.

From these points it should be clear that the Constitution was not rooted in the assumption that direct democracy was the ideal, to be replaced by republican institutions only because direct democracy was impractical in light of what were, by modern standards, extremely primitive technologies for communication. Many recent observers have suggested that for the first time in the history of the world, something like direct democracy has become feasible. It is now possible for citizens to tell their government, every week and even every day, what they would like it to do. Indeed, some websites have been designed to enable citizens to do precisely that. We should expect many more experiments in this direction. But from the standpoint of constitutional ideals, this is nothing to celebrate; indeed it is a grotesque distortion of founding aspirations. It would undermine the deliberative goals of the original design. Ours has never been a direct democracy, and a good democratic system attempts to ensure informed and reflective decisions, not simply snapshots of individual opinions suitably aggregated.[12]

Homogeneity, Heterogeneity, and a
Tale of the First Congress

There were articulate opponents of the original constitutional plan, whose voices have echoed throughout American history; and they spoke in terms that bear directly on the communications revolution. The anti-federalists believed that the Constitution was doomed to failure, on the ground that deliberation would not be possible in a large, heterogeneous republic. Following the great political theorist Montesquieu, they urged that public deliberation would be possible only where there was fundamental agreement. Thus Brutus, an eloquent anti-federalist critic of the Constitution, insisted: "In a republic, the manners, sentiments, and interests of the people should be similar, if this be not the case, there will be a constant clashing of opinions; and the representatives of one part will be continually striving against those of the other."[13]

It was here that the Constitution's framers made a substantial break with conventional republican thought, focusing on the potential uses of diversity for democratic debate. Indeed, it is here that we can find the framers' greatest and most original contribution to political theory. For them, heterogeneity, far from being an obstacle, would be a creative force, improving deliberation and producing better outcomes. If everyone agreed, what would people need to talk about? Why would they want to talk at all? Alexander Hamilton invoked this point to defend discussion among diverse people within a bicameral legislature, urging, in what could be taken as a direct response to Brutus, that "the jarring of parties . . . will promote delibera-

35

tion."[14] And in an often forgotten episode in the very first Congress, the nation rejected a proposed part of the original Bill of Rights, a "right" on the part of citizens "to instruct" their representative on how to vote. The proposed right was justified on republican (what we would call democratic) grounds. To many people, it seemed a good way of ensuring accountability on the part of public officials. But the early Congress decided that such a "right" would be a betrayal of republican principles. Senator Roger Sherman's voice was the clearest and most firm: "[T]he words are calculated to mislead the people, by conveying an idea that they have a right to control the debates of the Legislature. This cannot be admitted to be just, because it would destroy the object of their meeting. I think, when the people have chosen a representative, it is his duty to meet others from the different parts of the Union, and consult, and agree with them on such acts as are for the general benefit of the whole community. If they were to be guided by instructions, there would be no use in deliberation."[15]

Sherman's words reflect the founders' general receptivity to deliberation among people who are quite diverse and who disagree on issues both large and small. Indeed, it was through deliberation among such persons that "such acts as are for the general benefit of the whole community" would emerge. Of course the framers were not naïve. Sometimes some regions, and some groups, would gain while others would lose. What was and remains important is that the resulting pattern of gains and losses would themselves have to be defended by reference to reasons. Indeed, the Constitution might well be seen as intended to create a "republic of reasons," in which the use of governmental power would have to be justified, not simply supported, by those who asked for it.

We can even take Sherman's understanding of the task of the representative to have a corresponding understanding of the task of the idealized citizen in a well-functioning republic. Citizens are not supposed merely to press their own self-interest, narrowly conceived, nor are they to insulate themselves from the judgments of others. Even if they are concerned with the public good, they might make errors of fact or of value, errors that can be reduced or corrected through the exchange of ideas. Insofar as people are acting in their capacity as citizens, their duty is to "meet others" and "consult," sometimes through face-to-face discussions, and if not, through other routes, as, for example, by making sure to consider the views of those who think differently.

This is not to say that most people should be devoting most of their time to politics. In a free society, people have a range of things to do. But to the extent that both citizens and representatives are acting on the basis of diverse encounters and experiences and benefiting from heterogeneity, they are behaving in accordance with the highest ideals of the constitutional design.

E Pluribus Unum and Jefferson vs. Madison

Any heterogeneous society faces a risk of fragmentation. This risk has been serious in many periods in American history, most notably during the Civil War, but often in the twentieth century as well. The institutions of the Constitution were intended to diminish the danger, partly by producing a good mix of local and national rule, partly through the system of checks and balances, and partly through the symbol of the Constitution itself. Thus the slogan *e pluribus unum*, "from many, one," can be found on ordinary currency, in a brief, frequent reminder of a central constitutional goal.

37

Consider in this regard the instructive debate between Thomas Jefferson and James Madison about the value of a bill of rights. In the founding era, Madison, the most important force behind the Constitution itself, sharply opposed such a bill, on the ground that it was unnecessary and was likely to sow confusion. Jefferson thought otherwise, and insisted that a bill of rights, enforced by courts, could be a bulwark of liberty. Madison was eventually convinced of this point, but he emphasized a very different consideration: the unifying and educative functions of a bill of rights.

In a letter to Jefferson on October 17, 1788, Madison asked, "What use, then, it may be asked, can a bill of rights serve in popular Government?" His basic answer was that the "political truths declared in that solemn manner acquire by degrees the character of fundamental maxims of free Government, and as they become incorporated with the National sentiment, counteract the impulses of interest and passion."[16] In Madison's view, the Bill of Rights, along with the Constitution itself, would eventually become a source of shared understandings and commitments among extremely diverse people. The example illustrates the founders' belief that for a diverse people to be self-governing, it was essential to provide a range of common values and commitments.

Two Conceptions of Sovereignty
and Holmes vs. Brandeis

We are now in a position to distinguish between two conceptions of sovereignty. The first involves consumer sovereignty—the idea behind free markets. The second involves political sovereignty—the idea behind free nations. The notion of consumer sovereignty underlies enthusiasm for the Daily Me; it is the underpinning of any utopian vision of the unlimited power to filter. Writing as early as 1995, Bill Gates cheerfully predicted, "Customized information is a natural extension. . . . For your own daily dose of news, you might subscribe to several review services and let a software agent or a human one pick and choose from them to compile your completely customized 'newspaper.' These subscription services, whether human or electronic, will gather information that conforms to a particular philosophy and set of interests."[17]

Gates's prediction has now become a reality. With RSS, and many other services, you can gather information that fits your interests and your preexisting views. Or consider Gates's celebratory words in 1999: "When you turn on DirectTV and you step through every channel—well, there's three minutes of your life. When you walk into your living room six years from now, you'll be able to just say what you're interested in, and have the screen help you pick out a video that you care about. It's not going to be 'Let's look at channels 4, 5, and 7.'"[18]

This is the principle of consumer sovereignty in action. The notion of political sovereignty underlies the democratic alternative, which poses a challenge to this vision on the ground that it might undermine both self-government and freedom, properly conceived. Recall here John Dewey's words: "Majority rule, just as majority rule, is as foolish as its critics charge it with being. But it never is *merely* majority rule. . . . The important consideration is that opportunity be given ideas to speak and to become the possession of the multitude. The essential need is the improvement of the methods and constitution of debate, discussion and persuasion. That is *the* problem of the public."[19]

Consumer sovereignty means that individual consumers are permitted to choose exactly as they wish, subject to any constraints provided by the price system, and also by their

current holdings and requirements. This idea plays a significant role in thinking not only about economic markets, but
also about both politics and communications as well. When
we talk as if politicians are "selling" a message, and even
themselves, we are treating the political domain as a kind of
market, subject to the forces of supply and demand. And
when we act as if the purpose of a system of communications
is to ensure that people can see exactly what they "want," the
notion of consumer sovereignty is very much at work. The
idea of political sovereignty stands on different foundations.
It does not take individual tastes as fixed or given; it does
not see people as simply "having" tastes and preferences. For
those who value political sovereignty, "We the People" reflect
on what we want by exchanging diverse information and perspectives. The idea of political sovereignty embodies democratic self-government, understood as a requirement of "government by discussion," accompanied by reason giving in the
public domain. Political sovereignty comes with its own distinctive preconditions, and these are violated if government
power is not backed by justifications and represents instead
the product of force or simple majority will.

Of course the two conceptions of sovereignty are in potential tension. If laws and policies are "bought," in the same way
that soap and cereal are bought, the idea of political sovereignty is badly compromised. The commitment to consumer
sovereignty will also undermine political sovereignty if free
consumer choices result in insufficient understanding of
public problems, or if they make it difficult to have anything
like a shared or deliberative culture. We will disserve our own
aspirations if we confound consumer sovereignty with political sovereignty. If the latter is our governing ideal, we will
evaluate the system of free expression at least partly by seeing
whether it promotes democratic goals. If we care only about

40

consumer sovereignty, the only question is whether consumers are getting what they want—a question that seems, unfortunately, to be dominating discussions of the Internet and other new technologies.

The distinction matters for law and policy as well. If the government takes steps to increase the level of substantive debate on television or in public culture, it might well be undermining consumer sovereignty at the same time that it is promoting democratic self-government. And if citizens themselves urge that we ought to try to evaluate the system of communications by reference to democratic ideals, they ought not to be silenced on the ground that consumer sovereignty is all that matters.

With respect to the system of freedom of speech, the conflict between consumer sovereignty and political sovereignty can be found in an unexpected place: the great constitutional dissents of Supreme Court Justices Oliver Wendell Holmes and Louis Brandeis. In the early part of the twentieth century, Holmes and Brandeis were the twin heroes of freedom of speech, dissenting, usually together, from Supreme Court decisions allowing the government to restrict political dissent. Sometimes Holmes wrote for the two dissenters; sometimes the author was Brandeis. But the two spoke in quite different terms. Holmes wrote of "free trade in ideas," and treated speech as part of a great political market, with which government could not legitimately interfere. Consider a passage from Holmes's greatest free-speech opinion:

> [W]hen men have realized that time has upset many fighting faiths, they may come to believe even more than they believe the very foundations of their own conduct that the ultimate good desired is better reached by free trade in ideas—that the best test of truth is the power of the thought to get itself accepted in

the competition of the market, and that truth is the only ground upon which their wishes safely can be carried out. That at any rate is the theory of our Constitution.[20]

Brandeis's language, in his greatest free-speech opinion, was altogether different:

> Those who won our independence believed that the final end of the state was to make men free to develop their faculties; and that in its government the deliberative forces should prevail over the arbitrary. . . . They believed that . . . without free speech and assembly discussion would be futile; . . . that the greatest menace to freedom is an inert people; that public discussion is a political duty; and that this should be a fundamental principle of the American government.[21]

Note Brandeis's suggestion that the greatest threat to freedom is an "inert people," and his insistence, altogether foreign to Holmes, that public discussion is not only a right but "a political duty." Brandeis sees self-government as something dramatically different from an exercise in consumer sovereignty. Brandeis's conception of free speech is self-consciously republican, with its emphasis on the obligation to engage in public discussion. On the republican conception, unrestricted consumer choice is not an appropriate foundation for policy in a context where the very formation of preferences and the organizing processes of the democratic order are at stake.

In fact Brandeis can be taken to have offered a conception of the social role of the idealized citizen. For such a citizen, active engagement in politics, at least some of the time, is a responsibility, not just an entitlement. If citizens are "inert," freedom itself is at risk. If people are constructing a Daily Me that is restricted to sports or to the personal lives of celebrities, they are not operating in the way that citizenship requires. This does not mean that people have to be thinking about public affairs all, most, or even much of the time. But it does mean that each of us has rights and duties as citizens, not simply as consumers. As we will see, active citizen engagement is necessary to promote not only democracy but social well-being too. And in the modern era, one of the most pressing obligations of a citizenry that is not inert is to ensure that "deliberative forces should prevail over the arbitrary." For this to happen, it is indispensable to ensure that the system of communications promotes democratic goals. Those goals emphatically require both unchosen exposures and shared experiences.

Brandeis was speaking of the republican tradition. It is therefore noteworthy, and not a little comical, that republic.com is actually a website. Republic.com has nothing to do with republicanism as a political ideal. Instead it offers to sell you essentially whatever you want, as signaled by its distinctive motto: "What you need, when you need it." Its main offerings include women's clothing, airline tickets, T-shirts, designer clothes, houses for sale, hotels, and leather jackets. Republic.com offers an important service, to be sure, but it is not exactly following in the footsteps of its republican forbears.

Republicanism without Nostalgia

These are abstractions; it is time to be more concrete. I will identify three problems in the hypothesized world of perfect filtering. These difficulties might well beset any system in which individuals had complete control over their communications universe and exercised that control so as to create echo chambers or information cocoons.

The first difficulty involves *fragmentation*. The problem here comes from the creation of diverse speech communities whose members talk and listen mostly to one another. A possible consequence is considerable difficulty in mutual understanding. When society is fragmented in this way, diverse groups will tend to *polarize* in a way that can breed extremism and even hatred and violence. New technologies, emphatically including the Internet, are dramatically increasing people's ability to hear echoes of their own voices and to wall themselves off from others. An important result is the existence of *cybercascades*—processes of information exchange in which a certain fact or point of view becomes widespread, simply because so many people seem to believe it.

The second difficulty involves a distinctive characteristic of information. Information is a public good in the technical sense that once one person knows something, other people are likely to benefit as well. If you learn about crime in the neighborhood or about the problem of climate change, you might well tell other people too, and they will benefit from what you have learned. In a system in which each person can "customize" his own communications universe, there is a risk that people will make choices that generate too little information. An advantage of a system with general-interest intermediaries and with public forums—with broad access by speakers to diverse publics—is that it ensures a kind of social spreading of information. At the same time, an individually filtered speech universe is likely to produce too few of what I will call *solidarity goods*—goods whose value increases with the number of people who are consuming them.[22] A presidential debate is a classic example of a solidarity good.

The third and final difficulty has to do with the proper understanding of freedom and the relationship between consumers and citizens. If we believe in consumer sovereignty, and if we celebrate the power to filter, we are likely to think that freedom consists in the satisfaction of private preferences—in an absence of restrictions on individual choices. This is a widely held view about freedom. Indeed, it is a view that underlies much current thinking about free speech. But it is badly misconceived. Of course free choice is important. But freedom properly understood consists not simply in the satisfaction of whatever preferences people have, but also in the chance to have preferences and beliefs formed under decent conditions—in the ability to have preferences formed after exposure to a sufficient amount of information and also to an appropriately wide and diverse range of options. There can be no assurance of freedom in a system committed to the Daily Me.

3

Polarization and
Cybercascades

THERE is a discussion group on the Internet. The group was
started two years ago by about a dozen political activists who
were concerned about the increasing public pressure for gun
control and the perceived "emasculation" of the Second
Amendment (which, in the group's view, clearly bans government restrictions on the sale of guns). But the group was also
troubled by the growing authority of government, especially
the national government, over the lives of ordinary people,
and worried as well about the threat to our "European heritage" and to "traditional moral values" that is posed by uncon-
trolled immigration, by terrorism, by "Islamofascism," and by
the increasing social power of African Americans and "radical
feminist women." The group's members were fearful that the
Republican and Democratic Parties had become weak-willed
"twins," unable and unwilling to police national borders or to
take on the "special interests" who were threatening to "take
away our constitutional liberties." The group called itself the
Boston Tea Party.

The members of the Boston Tea Party now number well
over eight hundred people, who regularly exchange facts and
points of view, and who share relevant literature with one another. For a majority of the participants, the discussion group

provides most of the information on which they base their judgments about political issues. Over the last two years the Boston Tea Party's concerns have been greatly heightened. Nearly 70 percent of the members carry firearms, some as a result of the group's discussions. Small but vigorous protests have been planned, organized, and carried out in three state capitals. A march on Washington is now in the works. Recent discussion has occasionally turned to the need for "self-protection" against illegal immigrants, terrorists, and the state, through civil disobedience and possibly through selective "strikes" on certain targets in the public and private sectors. The motivation for this discussion is the widely disseminated view that the "FBI and possibly the CIA" are starting to take steps to "dismember" the group. One member has sent bomb-making instructions to all the other members of the Boston Tea Party. No violence has occurred as yet. But things are unquestionably heading in that direction.

So far as I know, there is no Boston Tea Party. This story is not true. But it is not exactly false. It is a composite based on the many discussion groups and websites, less and often more extreme, that can be found on the Internet. Discussion groups and websites of this kind have been around for a number of years. Not many years ago, for example, the *Terrorist's Handbook* was posted on the Internet, including instructions on how to make a bomb (the same bomb, as it happens, as was used in the Oklahoma City bombing, where dozens of federal employees were killed). On the National Rifle Association's "Bullet 'N' Board," a place for discussion of matters of mutual interest, someone calling himself "Warmaster" explained how to make bombs out of ordinary household materials. Warmaster explained, "These simple, powerful bombs are not very well known even though all the materials can be easily obtained by anyone (including minors)." After the

Oklahoma City bombing, an anonymous notice was posted not to one but to dozens of Usenet news groups, listing all the materials in the Oklahoma City bomb and exploring ways to improve future bombs.

Terrorists and hate groups have long been communicating on the Internet, often about conspiracies and (this will come as no surprise) formulas for making bombs. Members of such groups tend to communicate largely or mostly with one another, feeding their various predilections. The two students who launched the attack in Littleton, Colorado actually had an Internet site containing details about how to make a bomb. Often such sites receive and spread rumors, many of them false and even paranoid. The Bush administration's effort to monitor Internet traffic involving terrorism has been extremely controversial as a matter of both law and policy. But we should not doubt the claim that the Internet is sometimes used as a method for terrorists to communicate with one another.

Of course these are extreme cases. But they reveal something about the potential consequences of a fragmented speech market. In a system with robust public forums and general-interest intermediaries, self-insulation is more difficult, and people will frequently come across views and materials that they would not have chosen in advance. For diverse citizens, this provides something like a common framework for social experience. "Real-world interactions often force us to deal with diversity, whereas the virtual world may be more homogeneous, not in demographic terms, but in terms of interest and outlook. Place-based communities may be supplanted by interest-based communities."[1] Consider here the finding that communities who believe that the apocalypse is near, and who thought that the attacks of September 11 were a clear sign to that effect, used the Internet so as "to insulate" themselves "from the necessarily divergent ideas that might generate more constructive public discussion."[2]

Of course the Internet can bring people together rather than drawing them apart. Countless people are using the Internet to build larger and more diverse communities. But let us suppose that many other people are using the Internet in exactly the sense prophesied by those who celebrate the Daily Me, and in a way that invites the continuing emergence of highly specialized websites and discussion groups of innumerable sorts.

What problems would be created as a result?

Flavors and Filters

It is obvious that if there is only one flavor of ice cream, and only one kind of toaster, a wide range of people will make the same choice. (Some people will refuse ice cream, and some will rely on something other than toasters, but that is another matter.) It is also obvious that as choice is increased, different individuals and different groups will make increasingly different choices. This has been the growing pattern over time with the proliferation of communications options. Consider the remarkable rise of YouTube—the site that allows people to bypass general-interest intermediaries to show their own video clips, and to choose among an astonishing number of possibilities. Like-minded people can, in a sense, congregate to discuss and focus on one or more of those possibilities—not least when the clip casts ridicule on a particular person or point of view. Or consider the celebratory words of David Bohnett, founder of geocities.com: "The Internet gives you the opportunity to meet other people who are interested in the same things you are, no matter how specialized, no matter

49

how weird, no matter how big or how small."[3] This is un-doubtedly true, but it is not only an occasion for celebration.

To see this point, it is necessary to think a bit about why people are likely to engage in filtering. The simplest reason is that people often know, or think they know, what they like and dislike. A friend of mine is interested in Russia; he sub-scribes to a service that provides him with about two dozen stories about Russia each day. If you are bored by news stories involving Russia, or the Middle East, or if you have no interest in Wall Street, you might turn your mind off when these are discussed; and if you can filter your communications uni-verse accordingly, you might think that it's all the better. In addition, many people like hearing discussions that come from a perspective that they find sympathetic. If you are a Republican, you might prefer a newspaper with a Republican slant, or at least without a Democratic slant. And indeed, many Americans with conservative leanings prefer to get their news from avowedly conservative sources, whereas many Americans with liberal leanings work hard to avoid those sources.

Perhaps you are most willing to trust, and most enjoy, "ap-propriately slanted" stories about the events of the day. Your particular choices are designed to ensure that you can trust what you read. Or maybe you want to insulate yourself from opinions that you find implausible, indefensible, or invidious. Everyone considers some points of view beyond the pale, and we filter those out if this is at all possible. A personal confes-sion: I like the Chicago Bears, and when they are on national television, I turn off the sound and listen to the local an-nouncers. I do this not only because they are better, but also because they are biased in the Bears' favor; and when the Bears do badly, their hearts break along with mine. Or con-sider the fact that after people buy a new car, they often love to read advertisements that speak enthusiastically about the very car that they have just obtained. The reason is that those advertisements tend to be comforting because they confirm the wisdom of the decision.

We can make some distinctions here. Members of some groups want to wall themselves off from most or all others simply in order to maintain a degree of comfort and possibly a way of life. Some religious groups self-segregate for this reason. Such groups are tolerant of pluralism and interested largely in self-protection; they do not have large ambitions or seek to proselytize to others. Other groups have a self-conscious social project or even a kind of "combat mission" that seeks to convert others, and their desire to self-segregate is intended to strengthen their members' convictions in order to promote long-term recruitment and conversion plans. Terrorists operate in just this way. Political parties sometimes think in similar terms, and they often ignore the views of others, except when they hold those views up to ridicule. When links are provided to other sites, it is often to show how dangerous, or how contemptible, competing views really are. Bloggers routinely do exactly this.

Overload, Groupism, and *E Pluribus Plures*

In the face of dramatic recent increases in communications options, there is an omnipresent risk of information overload—too many options, too many topics, too many opinions, a cacophony of voices. Indeed the risk of overload and the need for filtering go hand in hand. Bruce Springsteen's music may be timeless, but his hit from the 1990s, "57 Channels and Nothing On," is hopelessly out of date in light of the number of current programming options, certainly if we take account

51

of the Internet. (Contradicting Springsteen, TiVo exclaims, "There's always something on TV that you'll like!") Filtering, often in the form of narrowing, is inevitable in order to avoid overload, to impose some order on an overwhelming number of sources of information.

By itself this is not a problem. But when options are so plentiful, many people will take the opportunity to listen to those points of view that they find most agreeable. For many of us, of course, what matters is that we enjoy what we see or read, or learn from it, and it is not necessary that we are comforted by it. But there is a natural human tendency to make choices with respect to entertainment and news that do not disturb our preexisting view of the world.

I am not suggesting that the Internet is a lonely or anti-social domain. In contrast to television, many of the emerging technologies are extraordinarily social, increasing people's capacity to form bonds with individuals and groups that would otherwise have been entirely inaccessible. Email, instant messaging, texting, and Internet discussion groups provide increasingly remarkable opportunities, not for isolation, but for the creation of new groups and connections. This is the foundation for the concern about the risk of fragmentation.

Consider in this regard a lovely little experiment.[4] Members of a nationally representative group of Americans were asked whether they would like to read news stories from one of four sources: Fox (known to be conservative), National Public Radio (known to be liberal), CNN (often thought to be liberal), and the British Broadcasting Network (whose politics are not widely known to Americans). The stories came in different news categories: American politics, the war in Iraq, "race in America," crime, travel, and sports. It turns out that for the first four categories, Republicans chose Fox by an overwhelming margin. By contrast, Democrats split their "votes" among National Public Radio and CNN—and showed a general aversion to Fox. For travel and sports, the divide between Republicans and Democrats was much smaller. By contrast, independents showed no preference for any particular source.

There was another finding, perhaps a more striking one: *people's level of interest in the same news stories was greatly affected by the network label.* For Republicans, the identical headline became far more interesting, and the story became far more attractive, if it carried the Fox label. In fact the Republican "hit rate" for the same news stories was three times higher when it was labeled "Fox"! (Interestingly, the hit rate was doubled when sports and travel stories were so labeled.) Democrats showed a real aversion to stories labeled "Fox," and the CNN and NPR labels created a modest increase in their interest. The overall conclusion is that Fox attracts substantial Republican support and that Democratic viewers and readers take pains to avoid Fox—while CNN and National Public Radio have noticeable but weak brand loyalty among Democrats. This is only one experiment, to be sure, but there is every reason to suspect that the result would generalize— that people with identifiable leanings are consulting sources, including websites, that match their predilections, and are avoiding sources that do not cater to those predilections.

All this is just the tip of the iceberg. "Because the Internet makes it easier to find like-minded individuals, it can facilitate and strengthen fringe communities that have a common ideology but are dispersed geographically. Thus, particle physicists, Star Trek fans, and members of militia groups have used the Internet to find each other, swap information and stoke each others' passions. In many cases, their heated dialogues might never have reached critical mass as long as geographical separation diluted them to a few parts per million."[5] It is worth underlining the idea that people are working to "stoke each others' passions," because that idea will play a large role in the discussion to follow. Of course many of those with committed views on one or another topic—gun control, abortion, affirmative action—are speaking mostly with each other. Linking behavior follows a similar pattern (as we shall see, with respect to blogs, in chapter 6).

My own study, conducted with Lesley Wexler in 2000, found the same basic picture. Of a random study of 60 political sites, only 9, or 15 percent, provided links to sites of those with opposing views, whereas 35, or almost 60 percent, provided links to like-minded sites. The basic findings are summarized in table 3.1.

Table 3.1

Links to Allies and Adversaries, 2000

Political orientation	Links to opposition	No links to opposition	Links to like-minded sites	No links to like-minded sites	Total sites
Republican	3	7	7	3	10
Democrats	1	11	7	5	12
Conservative	1	20	12	9	21
Liberal	4	13	9	8	17
All	9	51	35	25	60

In November 2006, Spencer Short and I did a follow-up study, which found a similar basic picture. Of a random study of 50 political sites, only 17, or 34 percent, provide links to sites of those with opposing views, whereas 41, or almost 82 percent, provide links to like-minded sites. The basic findings are summarized in table 3.2.

Table 3.2
Links to Allies and Adversaries, 2006

Political orientation	Links to opposition	No links to opposition	Links to like-minded sites	No links to like-minded sites	Total sites
Republican	3	7	7	3	10
Democrats	5	5	5	5	10
Conservative	3	13	16	0	14
Liberal	6	8	13	1	14
All	17	32	41	9	50

One of the most striking facts here is that when links to opposing sites are provided, it is often to show how dangerous, dumb, or contemptible the views of the adversary really are. Even more striking is the extent to which sites are providing links to like-minded sites. Tables 3.1 and 3.2 show the number of sites that have one or more such link, but in a way they greatly understate what is happening. Several organizations, for example, offer links to dozens or even hundreds of like-minded sites.

All this is perfectly natural, even reasonable. Those who visit certain sites are probably more likely to want to visit similar sites, and people who create a site with one point of view are unlikely to want to promote their adversaries. (Recall that collaborative filtering works because people tend to like what people like them tend to like.) And of course it is true that many people who consult sites with one point of view do not restrict themselves to like-minded sources of information. But what we now know about both links and individual behavior supports the general view that many people are mostly hearing more and louder echoes of their own voices. To say the least, this is undesirable from the democratic standpoint.

I do not mean to deny the obvious fact that any system that allows for freedom of choice will create some balkanization of opinion. Long before the advent of the Internet, and in an era of a handful of television stations, people made self-conscious choices among newspapers and radio stations. In any era, many people want to be comforted rather than challenged. Magazines and newspapers, for example, often cater to people with definite interests in certain points of view. Since the early nineteenth century, African American newspapers have been widely read by African Americans, and these newspapers offer significantly different coverage of common issues than white-oriented newspapers and also make dramatically different choices about what issues are important.[6] Whites rarely read such newspapers.

But what is emerging nonetheless counts as a significant change. With a dramatic increase in options, and a greater power to customize, comes a corresponding increase in the range of actual choices, and those choices are likely, in many cases, to match demographic characteristics, preexisting political convictions, or both. Of course this has many advantages; among other things, it will greatly increase the aggregate amount of information, the entertainment value of choices, and the sheer fun of the options. But there are problems as well. If diverse groups are seeing and hearing quite different points of view, or focusing on quite different topics, mutual understanding might be difficult, and it might be increasingly hard for people to solve problems that society faces together.

Take some extreme examples. Many Americans fear that certain environmental problems—abandoned hazardous waste sites, genetic engineering of food, climate change—are extremely serious and require immediate government action. But others believe that the same problems are imaginative fictions, generated by zealots and self-serving politicians. Many Americans think that most welfare recipients are indolent and content to live off of the work of others. On this view, "welfare reform," to be worthy of the name, consists of reduced handouts, a step necessary to encourage people to fend for themselves. But many other Americans believe that welfare recipients generally face severe disadvantages and would be entirely willing to work if decent jobs were available. On this view, welfare reform, understood as reductions in benefits, is an act of official cruelty. Many people believe that the largest threat to American security remains terrorism, and that if terrorism is not a top priority, catastrophic attacks are likely to ensue. Many others believe that while terrorism presents serious risks, the threat has been overblown, and that other problems, including climate change, deserve at least equal attention.

To say the least, it will be difficult for people armed with such opposing perspectives to reach anything like common ground or to make progress on the underlying questions. Consider how these difficulties will increase if people do not know the competing view, consistently avoid speaking with one another, and are unaware how to address divergent concerns of fellow citizens.

A Brief Note on Hate Groups

As noted, there are hundreds of websites created and run by hate groups and extremist organizations. They appear to be achieving a measure of success, at least if we measure this by reference to "hits." Some such groups have had hundreds of thousands or even millions of visitors. What is also striking is that many extremist organizations and hate groups provide links to one another, and expressly attempt to encourage both recruitment and discussion among like-minded people.

Consider one extremist group, the so-called Unorganized Militia, the armed wing of the Patriot movement, "which believes that the federal government is becoming increasingly dictatorial with its regulatory power over taxes, guns and land use."[7] A crucial factor behind the growth of the Unorganized Militia "has been the use of computer networks," allowing members "to make contact quickly and easily with like-minded individuals to trade information, discuss current conspiracy theories, and organize events."[8] In the recent past, the Unorganized Militia has had a large number of websites, and those sites frequently offered links to related sites. It is clear that websites are being used to recruit new members as well as to allow like-minded people to speak with one another and to reinforce or strengthen existing convictions. It is also clear that the Internet is playing a crucial role in permitting people who would otherwise feel isolated, or move on to something else, to band together and spread rumors, many of them paranoid and hateful.

There are numerous other examples along similar lines. Consider a few examples from the recent past. A group naming itself the "White Racial Loyalists" called on all "White Racial Loyalists to go to chat rooms and debate and recruit with NEW people, post our URL everywhere, as soon as possible." Another site announced that "Our multi-ethnic United States is run by Jews, a 2 percent minority, who were run out of every country in Europe. . . . Jews control the U.S. media, they hold top positions in the Clinton administration . . . and now these Jews are in control—they used lies spread by the media they run and committed genocide in our name." Table 3.3 gives a brief snapshot of what is out there.

Table 3.3
Links among "Hate Sites"

Site	Links to like-minded sites	Links to opposition
Adelaide institute (Holocaust revisionism)	39	5
Aggressive Christianity	1	0
Altar of Unholy Blasphemy	23	0
Aryan Nations	28	0
Crosstar (nationalistic)	5	0
David Duke Online	10	0
Islam-watch.org	88	0
Klassen's teachings (white supremacy)	41	0
Martin Luther King Jr (revisionist view of King)	0	0
Stormfront (white nationalism)	60	5
Tightrope	6	0
Vanguard News Network	11	0
Stormfront (white nationalism)	60	5
White Revolution Forum	13	0
Misogyny Unlimited	35	4
White Aryan Resistance	0	0
World Church of the Creator	11	0
Total Sites — 16	14 with 2 without	3 with 13 without

Here in particular, the provision of opposition links is designed not to produce discussion but instead fear and contempt. Holocaust-denial organizations, for example, describe their adversaries as "exterminationists" or "Holocaust enforcers" and provide links with the evident goal of discrediting them. With respect to like-minded sites, several hate groups have formal linking agreements: "You link to us and we'll link to you." One such site listed nearly a hundred such groups, each with a link, under the title "White Pride World Wide." The listed sites included European Knights of the Ku Klux Klan, German Skin Heads, Aryan Nations, Knights of the Ku Klux Klan, Siegheil88, Skinhead Pride, Intimidation One, SS Enterprises, and White Future.

Sites about the Islamic world have multiplied exponentially since September 11, 2001. For instance, islam-watch.org links to eighty-eight sites, all of them anti-Islam or pro-secularization, ranging from the anti-Islam blog Little Green Footballs, to amateur polemics, to the Human Rights Congress for Bangladeshi Minorities. One result of this kind of mass linking between sources of varying levels of professionalism and veracity is to blur the line between sometimes vitriolic attacks and much more responsible opinion writing.

We can sharpen our understanding here if we attend to the phenomenon of *group polarization*. This phenomenon raises serious questions about any system in which individuals and groups make diverse choices, and many people end up in echo chambers of their own design. On the Internet, polarization is a real phenomenon; we might even call it cyberpolarization. To understand how it works, we need to investigate a little social science.

Group Polarization in General

The term "group polarization" refers to something very simple: after deliberation, people are likely to move toward a more extreme point in the direction to which the group's members were originally inclined. With respect to the Internet and new communications technologies, the implication is that groups of like-minded people, engaged in discussion with one another, will end up thinking the same thing that they thought before—but in more extreme form.

For an initial glimpse of the problem, let us put the Internet to one side and consider a small experiment in democracy that was held in Colorado in 2005.[9] About sixty American citizens were brought together and assembled into ten groups, each consisting of six people. Members of each group were asked to deliberate on three of the most controversial issues of the day: *Should states allow same-sex couples to enter into civil unions? Should employers engage in "affirmative action" by giving a preference to members of traditionally disadvantaged groups? Should the United States sign an international treaty to combat global warming?*

As the experiment was designed, the groups consisted of "liberal" and "conservative" members—the former from Boulder, the latter from Colorado Springs. It is widely known that Boulder tends to be liberal and that Colorado Springs tends to be conservative. The groups were screened to ensure that their members conformed to these stereotypes. In the parlance of election years, there were five "blue state" groups and five "red state" groups—five groups whose members initially tended toward liberal positions on the three issues, and five whose members tended toward conservative positions on those issues. People were asked to state their opinions anonymously both before and after fifteen minutes of group discussion, and also to try to reach a public verdict before the final anonymous statement. What was the effect of discussion?

The results were simple. In almost every group, members ended up with more extreme positions after they spoke with one another. Discussion made civil unions more popular among liberals; discussion made civil unions less popular among conservatives. Liberals favored an international treaty to control global warming before discussion; they favored it

61

more strongly after discussion. Conservatives were neutral on that treaty before discussion; they strongly opposed it after discussion. Mildly favorable toward affirmative action before discussion, liberals became strongly favorable toward affirmative action after discussion. Firmly negative about affirmative action before discussion, conservatives became even more negative about affirmative action after discussion.

Aside from increasing extremism, the experiment also had an independent effect: it made both liberal groups and conservative groups significantly more homogeneous—and thus squelched diversity. Before members started to talk, many groups displayed a fair bit of internal disagreement. The disagreements were reduced as a result of a mere fifteen-minute discussion. Even in their anonymous statements, group members showed far more consensus after discussion than before. It follows that discussion helped to widen the rift between liberals and conservatives on all three issues. Before discussion, some liberal groups were, on some issues, fairly close to some conservative groups. The result of discussion was to divide them far more sharply.

The Colorado experiment is vivid evidence of group polarization, but the basic phenomenon has been found in over a dozen nations.[10] Consider a few examples:

- Members of a group of moderately profeminist women become more strongly profeminist after discussion.[11]
- After discussion, citizens of France become more critical of the United States and its intentions with respect to economic aid.[12]
- After discussion, whites predisposed to show racial prejudice offer more negative responses to the question of whether white racism is responsible for conditions faced by African Americans in American cities.[13]

- After discussion, whites predisposed not to show racial prejudice offer more positive responses to the same question.[14]
- Republican appointees, on three-judge panels, show especially conservative voting patterns when they sit only with fellow Republican appointees; Democratic appointees show especially liberal voting patterns when they sit only with fellow Democratic appointees.[15]

The phenomenon of group polarization has conspicuous importance for the communications market, where groups with distinctive identities increasingly engage in within-group discussion. Effects of the kind just described should be expected with terrorist and hate groups, as well as with less extreme organizations of all sorts. If the public is balkanized, and if different groups are designing their own preferred communications packages, the consequence will be not merely the same but still more balkanization, as group members move one another toward more extreme points in line with their initial tendencies. At the same time, different deliberating groups, each consisting of like-minded people, will be driven increasingly far apart, simply because most of their discussions are with one another.

It is true that many or most of us do not use the power to filter so as to wall ourselves off from other points of view. But even so, some or many people will do, and are doing, exactly that. This is sufficient for significant polarization to occur, and to cause serious social risks. In general, it is precisely the people most likely to filter out opposing views who most need to hear such views. New technologies, emphatically including the Internet, make it easier for people to surround themselves (virtually of course) with the opinions of like-minded but otherwise isolated others, and to insulate themselves from competing views. For this reason alone, they are a breeding ground for polarization, and potentially dangerous for both democracy and social peace.

Why Polarization?

There have been three main explanations for group polarization. Massive evidence now supports all three explanations.

Persuasive arguments and information. The first explanation emphasizes the role of persuasive arguments and information. The intuition here is simple: any individual's position on any issue is a function, at least in part, of which arguments seem convincing. If you are like most people, you are likely to pay attention to the information held and revealed by group members. And if your position is going to move as a result of group discussion, it is likely to move in the direction of the most persuasive position defended within the group, taken as a whole.

If the group's members are already inclined in a certain direction, they will offer a disproportionately large number of arguments tending in that same direction, and a disproportionately small number of arguments tending the other way. As a result, the consequence of discussion will be to move people further in the direction of their initial inclinations. Thus, for example, a group whose members lean in favor of the nation's current leader will, in discussion, provide a wide range of arguments in his favor, and the arguments made in opposition to him will be both fewer and weaker. The group's members, to the extent that they shift, will shift toward a more extreme position in favor of the current leader. And the group as a whole, if a group decision is required, will move not to the median position, but to a more extreme point.

On this account, the central factor behind group polarization is the existence of a *limited argument pool*, one that is skewed (speaking purely descriptively) in a particular direction. It is easy to see how shifts might happen with discussion groups on the Internet; consider a group of Democrats, or Socialists, or members of the Unorganized Militia, or terrorists, or environmentalists. Indeed, the same thing should occur with individuals not engaged in discussion but consulting only ideas—on radio, television, or the Internet—to which they are antecedently inclined. The tendency of such consultations will be to entrench and reinforce preexisting positions—often resulting in extremism. If people who watch Fox News are drawn further to the right, or if people who watch Al Jazeera end up with less enthusiasm for the United States, the relevant argument pool is probably playing a large role.

Social comparison. The second mechanism, involving social comparison, begins with the reasonable suggestion that people want to be perceived favorably by other group members, and also to perceive themselves favorably. Once they hear what others believe, they often adjust their positions in the direction of the dominant position. The German sociologist Elisabeth Noell-Neumann has used this idea as the foundation for a general theory of public opinion, involving a "spiral of silence" in which people with minority positions silence themselves, potentially excising those positions from society over time.[16]

Suppose, for example, that people in a certain group tend to be sharply opposed to a certain war, continued reliance on fossil fuels, and gun ownership, and that they also want to be seen to be sharply opposed to all these. If they are in a group whose members are also sharply opposed to these things, they might well shift in the direction of even sharper opposition

65

after they see what other group members think. In countless studies, exactly this pattern is observed. Of course people will not shift if they have a clear sense of what they think and are not movable by the opinions of others. But most people, most of the time, are not so fixed in their views.

The point offers an account of the likely effects of exposure to ideas and claims on television, radio, and the Internet— even in the absence of a chance for interaction. Note that group polarization occurs merely on the basis of exposure to the views of others. The "mere exposure" effect means that polarization is likely to be a common phenomenon in a balkanized speech market. Suppose, for example, that conservatives are visiting conservative sites; that liberals are visiting liberal sites; that environmentalists are visiting sites dedicated to establishing the risks of genetic engineering and global warming; that critics of environmentalists are visiting sites dedicated to exposing frauds allegedly perpetrated by environmentalists; that people inclined to racial hatred are visiting sites that express racial hatred. To the extent that these exposures are not complemented by exposure to competing views, group polarization will be the inevitable consequence.

Confidence, corroboration, and extremism. A final explanation of group polarization stresses the close links among confidence, extremism, and corroboration by others.[17] On many issues, people are really not sure what they think, and their lack of certainty inclines them toward the middle. As people gain confidence, they usually become more extreme in their beliefs. Agreement from others tends to increase confidence, and for this reason like-minded people, having deliberated with one another, become more sure that they are right and thus more extreme. In many contexts, involving the attractiveness of people in slides and the comfort of chairs, the opinions of ordinary people in experiments become more extreme simply because their views have been corroborated, and because they become more confident after learning that others share their views.[18]

If you learn that other "people like you" like a certain band, or a particular movie, or an identifiable political position, or a particular candidate, you might well follow their lead. Indeed, if you learn that "people like you" tend to have a certain position on national security, or on Social Security reform, you might well end up adopting their position, and perhaps doing so with great confidence, even if you haven't much thought about the question independently. Consider the fact that most Americans believe that the United States should ratify the Kyoto Protocol, designed to control global warming; but when they are told that President Bush opposes ratification, only 43 percent of Americans favor the protocol. Whatever we think of the Kyoto Protocol, it is clear that when people find that their initial inclination is shared by others, they often become more confident and more extreme.

The Enormous Importance of Group Identity

For purposes of understanding modern technologies and the nature of polarization on the Internet, perceptions of identity and group membership are particularly important to consider. Group polarization will significantly increase if people think of themselves, antecedently or otherwise, as part of a group having a shared identity and a degree of solidarity. If they think of themselves in this way, group polarization is both more likely and more extreme.[19] If, for example, a number of people in an Internet discussion group think of them-

67

selves as opponents of high taxes, or fans of Barack Obama, or advocates of animal rights, or critics of the Supreme Court, their discussions are likely to move them in quite extreme directions, simply because they understand each other as part of a common cause. Similar movements should be expected for those who listen to a radio show known to be conservative, or who watch a television program dedicated to traditional religious values or to exposing white racism. Considerable evidence so suggests.[20]

Group identity is important in another way. Suppose that you are participating in an Internet discussion group, but you think that other group members are significantly different from you. If so, you are less likely to be moved by what they say. If, for example, other group members are styled "Republicans," and you consider yourself a Democrat, you might not shift at all—even if you would indeed shift, as a result of the same arguments if you were all styled "voters" or "jurors" or "citizens." Thus a perception of shared group identity will heighten the effect of others' views, whereas a perception of unshared identity, and of relevant differences, will reduce that effect, and possibly even eliminate it.

These findings should not be surprising. Recall that in ordinary cases, group polarization is a product of limited argument pools, social comparisons, and the effects of corroboration. If this is so, it stands to reason that when group members think of one another as similar along a salient dimension, or if some external factor (politics, geography, race, sex) unites them, group polarization will be heightened. If identity is shared, persuasive arguments are likely to be still more persuasive; the identity of those who are making them gives them a kind of credential or boost. And if identity is shared, social influences will have still greater force. People do not like their reputations to suffer in the eyes of those who seem most like them. And if you think that group members are in some relevant sense different from you, their arguments are less likely to be persuasive, and social influences may not operate as much or at all. If "people like you" support your initial inclination, you will become more confident. But if your inclination is supported by "people not like you," you might become less confident, and start to rethink your position. If your political opponents—those whom you think most confused and destructive—think that your position is right, you might end up thinking that it is wrong.

Group Polarization and the Internet

Group polarization is unquestionably occurring on the Internet. From the evidence thus far, it seems plain that the Internet is serving, for many, as a breeding group for extremism, precisely because like-minded people are deliberating with greater ease and frequency with one another, and often without hearing contrary views. Repeated exposure to an extreme position, with the suggestion that many people hold that position, will predictably move those exposed, and likely predisposed, to believe in it. One consequence can be a high degree of fragmentation, as diverse people, not originally fixed in their views and perhaps not so far apart, end up in extremely different places, simply because of what they are reading and viewing. Another consequence can be a high degree of error and confusion. YouTube is a lot of fun, and in a way it is a genuine democratizing force; but there is a risk that isolated clips, taken out of context, will lead like-minded people to end up with a distorted understanding of some issue, person, or practice.

A number of studies have shown group polarization in Internet-like settings. An especially interesting experiment finds particularly high levels of polarization when group members met relatively anonymously and when group identity was emphasized.[21] From this experiment, it is reasonable to speculate that polarization is highly likely to occur, and to be extreme, under circumstances in which group membership is made salient and people have a high degree of anonymity. These are, of course, potential features of deliberation via the Internet.[22]

Consider in this regard a revealing study not of extremism, but of serious errors within working groups, both face-to-face and more importantly online.[23] The purpose of the study was to see how groups might collaborate to make personnel decisions. Resumes for three candidates applying for a marketing manager position were placed before the several groups. The attributes of the candidates were rigged by the experimenters so that one applicant was clearly best matched for the job described. Packets of information, each containing only a subset of information from the resumes, were given to the subjects, so that each group member had only part of the relevant information. The groups consisted of three people, some operating face-to-face, some operating online.

Two results were especially striking. First, group polarization was common, in the sense that groups ended up in a more extreme position in line with members' predeliberation views. Second, almost none of the deliberating groups made what was conspicuously the right choice! The reason is that they failed to share information in a way that would permit the group to make the correct decision. In online groups, the level of mistake was especially high, for the simple reason that members tended to share positive information about the emerging winning candidate and negative information about the losers while also suppressing negative information about the emerging winner and positive information about the emerging losers. These contributions served to "reinforce the march toward group consensus rather than add complications and fuel debate."[24] In fact this tendency was *twice* as large within the online groups. There is a warning here about the consequences of the Internet for democratic deliberation.

Of course it is true that many people are using the Internet to learn about competing positions, not merely to reinforce their existing tendencies. It is certainly possible for more information and less polarization to result from the increase in available sources. This is happening every day. But the study just described offers a clear warning. When people deliberate together, they often give disproportionate weight to "common knowledge"—information that they all share in advance. By contrast, they often give too little weight to unshared information—information that is held by one or only a few people.[25] There is every reason to think that the same asymmetry will be observed on the Internet.

Fragmentation, Polarization, Radio, and Television

An understanding of group polarization casts light on the potential effects not only of the Internet but also of radio and television, at least if stations are numerous and many take a well-defined point of view. Recall that mere exposure to the positions of others creates group polarization. It follows that this effect will be at work for nondeliberating groups, in the form of collections of individuals whose communications choices go in the same direction, and who do not expose themselves to alternative positions. Indeed the same process is likely to occur for newspaper choices. If some people are

71

reading the liberal newspaper, and others are reading the conservative newspaper, polarization is inevitable. When they are working well, general-interest intermediaries have a distinctive role here, by virtue of their effort to present a wide range of topics and views. Polarization is far less likely to occur when such intermediaries dominate the scene. A similar point can be made about the public-forum doctrine. When diverse speakers have access to a heterogeneous public, individuals and groups are less likely to be able to insulate themselves from competing positions and concerns. Fragmentation is correspondingly less likely.

Group polarization also raises more general issues about communications policy. Consider the "fairness doctrine," now largely abandoned but once requiring radio and television broadcasters to devote time to public issues and to allow an opportunity for opposing views to speak. The latter prong of the doctrine was designed to ensure that listeners would not be exposed to any single view. If one view was covered, the opposing position would have to be allowed a right of access. When the Federal Communications Commission abandoned the fairness doctrine, it did so on the grounds that this second prong led broadcasters, much of the time, to avoid controversial issues entirely, and to present views in a way that suggested a bland uniformity. Subsequent research has suggested that the elimination of the fairness doctrine has indeed produced a flowering of controversial substantive programming, frequently expressing extreme views of one kind or another; consider talk radio.[26]

Typically this is regarded as a story of wonderfully successful deregulation. The effects of eliminating the fairness doctrine were precisely what was sought and intended. But from the standpoint of group polarization, the evaluation is a bit more complicated. On the good side, the existence of diverse

72

pockets of opinion would seem to enrich society's total argument pool, potentially to the benefit of all of us. At the same time, the growth of a wide variety of issues-oriented programming—expressing strong, often extreme views, and appealing to dramatically different groups of listeners and viewers—is likely to create group polarization. All too many people are now exposed largely to louder echoes of their own voices, resulting, on occasion, in misunderstanding and enmity. Perhaps it is better for people to hear fewer controversial views than for them to hear a single such view, stated over and over again.

I do not suggest, or believe, that the fairness doctrine should be restored. Law professor Heather Gerken has rightly drawn attention to "second-order diversity"—the kind of diversity that comes when society consists of many institutions and groups, some of which have little in the way of internal diversity.[27] As Gerken has shown, we all can benefit from a decentralized system in which different groups have different predispositions and sometimes go to different extremes. Instead of seeking diversity *within* each group, we might want diverse groups, even if many or most show little internal diversity. So too for communications outlets. If some radio shows press quite conservative arguments, and others press quite liberal arguments, we might all be able to benefit from what emerges. But at the very least there is a risk, in the current situation, that too many people will be insulated from exposure to views that are more moderate, or extreme in another direction, or in any case different from their own.

Why They Hate Us: A Speculative Note

Since the attacks of September 11, 2001, many Americans have been focused on a simple question: *Why do they hate us?* We should now be able to see that part of the answer lies, not in anything particular to Islam, to religion, or even to the rhetoric of Osama Bin Ladin, but in social dynamics and especially in the process of group polarization. And in fact, leaders of terrorist organizations show a working knowledge of group polarization. They attempt to ensure that "recruits" speak mostly to people who are already predisposed in the preferred direction. There is no natural predisposition toward terrorism, even among the most disaffected people in the poorest nations. Social dynamics—not poverty, poor education, and disadvantage—play the key role.[28]

Terrorist leaders act as *polarization entrepreneurs*. They create enclaves of like-minded people. They stifle dissenting views and take steps to ensure a high degree of internal solidarity. Consider the following account:[29]

> Terrorists do not even consider that they may be wrong and that other views may have some merit. . . . They attribute only evil motives to anyone outside their group. The . . . common characteristic of the psychologically motivated terrorist is the pronounced need to belong to a group. . . . Such individuals define their social status by group acceptance. . . . Terrorist groups with strong internal motivations find it necessary to justify the group's existence continuously. A terrorist group must terrorize. As a minimum, it must commit violent acts to maintain group self-esteem and legitimacy. Thus, terrorists sometimes carry out attacks that are objectively nonproductive or even counterproductive to their announced goal.

In fact terrorist organizations impose psychological pressure to accelerate the movement in extreme directions. Thus:

> Another result of psychological motivation is the intensity of group dynamics among terrorists. They tend to demand una-

74

nimity and be intolerant of dissent. With the enemy clearly identified and unequivocally evil, pressure to escalate the frequency and intensity of operations is ever present. The need to belong to the group discourages resignations, and the fear of compromise disallows their acceptance. Compromise is rejected, and terrorist groups lean toward maximalist positions. . . . In societies in which people identify themselves in terms of group membership (family, clan, tribe), there may be a willingness to self-sacrifice seldom seen elsewhere.[30]

In the particular context of al Qaeda, there is a pervasive effort to link Muslims all over the globe, above all by emphasizing a shared identity, one that includes some and excludes others. Thus Bin Ladin "appeals to a pervasive sense of humiliation and powerlessness in Islamic countries. Muslims are victims the world over . . . Bosnia, Somalia, Palestine, Chechnya, and . . . Saudi Arabia. . . . He makes the world simple for people who are otherwise confused, and gives them a sense of mission."[31] Hence there are cultlike features to the indoctrination effort: "The military training [in al Qaeda camps] is accompanied by forceful religious indoctrination, with recruits being fed a stream of anti-western propaganda and being incessantly reminded about their duty to perform jihad."[32] In addition, the al Qaeda terrorists are taught to believe that they are "not alone . . . but sacrificing themselves as part of a larger group for what they believe is the greater good. [The men are] recruited as teenagers, when self-esteem and separation from family are huge developmental issues. [The indoctrination] involves not only lessons in weaponry but an almost cult-like brainwashing over many months. Among Muslims, the regimen typically includes extended periods of prayer and a distortion of the Koran."[33]

This regimen does not, of course, involve the Internet, and it would be ludicrous to attribute terrorism to new communications technologies. But there is no question that terrorism is fueled by some of the dynamics that I have been exploring here. It is possible to go further. Some Internet sites, and some communications outlets, are specifically designed to promote terrorism or at the very least to portray terrorists in a sympathetic light. Members of al Qaeda themselves use new technologies, including the Internet, to promote discussion among like-minded people. In this light we can see that terrorists and extremists often suffer from a kind of "crippled epistemology."[34] They know very little, and what they know comes in large part from people who appeal to, and amplify, their preexisting inclinations.

Is Group Polarization Bad? Of Enclave Deliberation

Of course we cannot always say, from the mere fact of group polarization, that there has been a movement in the *wrong* direction. Notwithstanding some of the grotesque examples given here, the more extreme tendency might be better rather than worse. Indeed, group polarization helped fuel many movements of great value— including, for example, the civil rights movement, the antislavery movement, and the movement for equality between men and women. All of these movements were extreme in their time, and within-group discussion certainly bred greater extremism; but extremism need not be a word of opprobrium. If greater communications choices produce greater extremism, society may be better off as a result. One reason is that when many different groups are deliberating with one another, society will hear a far wider range of views; recall the idea of second-order diversity. Even if the "information diet" of many individuals is homogeneous, or insufficiently diverse, society as a whole might have a richer and fuller set of ideas. This is another side of the general picture of social fragmentation. It suggests some large benefits from pluralism and diversity—benefits even if individuals customize and cluster in groups.

We might define *enclave deliberation* as that form of deliberation that occurs within more or less insulated groups, in which like-minded people speak mostly to one another. The Internet, along with other new communications options, makes it much easier to engage in enclave deliberation. It is obvious that enclave deliberation can be extremely important in a heterogeneous society, not least because members of some groups tend to be especially quiet when participating in broader deliberative bodies. In this light, a special advantage of enclave deliberation is that it promotes the development of positions that would otherwise be invisible, silenced, or squelched in general debate. The efforts of marginalized groups to exclude outsiders, and even of political parties to limit their primaries to party members, might be justified in similar terms. Even if group polarization is at work—perhaps *because* group polarization is at work—enclaves, emphatically including those produced by the Internet and other new technologies, can provide a wide range of social benefits, not least because they greatly enrich the social "argument pool."

The central empirical point here is that in deliberating bodies, high-status members tend to speak more than others, and their ideas are more influential—partly because low-status members lack confidence in their own abilities, and partly because they fear retribution.[35] For example, women's ideas are often less influential and sometimes are "suppressed altogether in mixed-gender groups."[36] In ordinary circumstances, cultural minorities have disproportionately little influence on decisions by culturally mixed groups. In light of the inevitable existence of some status-based hierarchies, it makes sense to be receptive to deliberating enclaves in which members of multiple groups may speak with one another and develop their views. The Internet is and will continue to be particularly valuable insofar as it makes this easier.

But there is also a serious danger in such enclaves. The danger is that through the mechanisms of persuasive arguments, social comparisons, and corroboration, members will move to positions that lack merit but are predictable consequences of the particular circumstances of enclave deliberation. In the extreme case, enclave deliberation may even put social stability at risk. And it is impossible to say, in the abstract, that those who sort themselves into enclaves will generally move in a direction that is desirable for society at large or even for its own members. It is easy to think of examples to the contrary, as, for example, in the rise of Nazism, hate groups, terrorists, and cults of various sorts.

Enclaves and a Public Sphere

Whenever group discussion tends to lead people to more strongly held versions of the same view with which they began, there is legitimate reason for concern. This does not mean that the discussions can or should be regulated. But it does raise questions about the idea that "more speech" is necessarily an adequate remedy for bad speech—especially if many people are inclined and increasingly able to wall themselves off from competing views. In democratic societies, the best response is suggested by the public-forum doctrine, whose most fundamental goal is to increase the likelihood that at certain points, there is an exchange of views between enclave members and those who disagree with them. It is total or near-total self-insulation, rather than group deliberation as such, that carries with it the most serious dangers, often in the highly unfortunate (and sometimes literally deadly) combination of extremism with marginality.[37]

To explore some of the advantageous of heterogeneity, let us engage in a thought experiment. Imagine a deliberating body consisting not of a subset of like-minded people, but of all citizens in the relevant group; this may mean all citizens in a community, a state, a nation, even the world. Imagine that through the magic of the computer, everyone can talk to everyone else. By hypothesis, the argument pool would be very large. It would be limited only to the extent that the set of citizen views was similarly limited. Of course social influences would remain. If you are one of a small minority of people who deny that global warming is a serious problem, you might decide to join the crowd. But when deliberation revealed to people that their private position was different, in relation to the group, from what they thought it was, any shift would be in response to an accurate understanding of all relevant citizens, and not a product of a skewed sample. And in fact, we can think of some online efforts as attempting to approximate this thought experiment. *Wikipedia*, for example, allows anyone to be an editor (within limits), and the theory is that countless people can contribute their dispersed information to produce a resource offering an immense amount of human knowledge. This largely successful effort, resulting in a single product to which all can contribute, might be compared with deliberating enclaves of like-minded people.

The thought experiment, or the *Wikipedia* example, does not suggest that a fragmented or balkanized speech market is always bad or that the hypothesized, all-inclusive deliberating body would be ideal. It would be foolish to suggest that all discussion should occur, even as an ideal, with all others. The great benefit of deliberating enclaves is that positions may emerge that otherwise would not, and that deserve to play a larger role both within the enclave and within the heterogeneous public. Properly understood, the case for deliberating enclaves is that they will improve social deliberation, democratic and otherwise, precisely because enclave deliberation is often required for incubating new ideas and perspectives that will add a great deal to public debate. But for these improvements to occur, members must not insulate themselves from competing positions. At the very least, any such attempt at insulation must not be a prolonged affair. The phenomenon of group polarization suggests that with respect to communications, consumer sovereignty might well produce serious problems for individuals and society at large—and these problems will occur by a kind of iron logic of social interaction.

Politics, Polarization, and Depolarization

It is no news that political candidates and their supporters are using the Internet to their advantage. What is perhaps more interesting is that candidates for public office and their supporters have also been using the Internet in a way that shows an intuitive understanding of group polarization. Their sites operate as "places" in which like-minded people might congregate and adopt shared positions about policies, adversaries, and their candidate. In a sense, candidates try to produce their own online version of the Colorado experiment, in which social interactions produce more consensus and more enthusiasm—eventually yielding both time and money. The mechanisms discussed here may or may not cause harm, but they can certainly be used strategically by those who are aware of them.

In certain circumstances, however, polarization can be decreased or even eliminated. No shift should be expected from people who are confident that they know what they think, and who are simply not going to be moved by what they hear from other people. If, for example, you are entirely sure of your position with respect to nuclear power—if you are confident not only of your precise view but of the degree of confidence with which you ought to hold it—the positions of other people will not affect you. People of this sort will not shift by virtue of any changes in the communications market.

I have mentioned that federal judges are prone to polarization—that Republican appointees show especially conservative voting patterns when sitting with fellow Republican appointees, and that Democratic appointees show especially liberal voting patterns when sitting with fellow Democratic appointees. But on two issues, federal judges appear to be uninfluenced by their peers: abortion and capital punishment.[38] On these issues, federal judges show essentially the same voting patterns regardless of whether they are sitting with zero, one, or two judges appointed by a president of the same political party as the president who appointed them. Apparently there is no polarization on abortion and capital punishment simply because judicial views are deeply held and entrenched. We can easily imagine other issues about which ordinary people are similarly unlikely to be affected by group members. In the political domain, polarization finds its limits here, whatever candidates attempt to do.

With artful design of deliberating groups, moreover, it is possible to produce *depolarization*—shifts toward the middle of the extremes. Suppose, for example, that a group of twelve people is constructed so as to include six people who have one view and six people who think the opposite—for example, half of the group's members believe that global warming is a serious problem, while the other half think that it is not. If most of the members do not have entirely fixed positions, there is likely to be real movement toward the middle. The persuasive-arguments view helps explain why this is so. By hypothesis, the "argument pool" includes an equal number of claims both ways. If people are willing to dismiss those who disagree with them, depolarization might not occur. A group consisting of three Israelis and three members of Hamas might not depolarize; group members might simply dismiss the views of those who disagree. But for many questions, people are likely to listen to one another and hence depolarization is possible.

Of course mixed groups are no panacea. Usually group members will end up at a more extreme point in line with the predeliberation median. No less than like-minded groups, mixed groups can polarize.[39] More generally, confronting opposing positions can dampen political participation, in part because people who become more ambivalent, and more uncertain about their own views, might simply stand to one side.[40] But mixed groups been shown to have two desirable effects. First, exposure to competing positions generally increases political tolerance.[41] After hearing a variety of views, including those that diverge from their own, many people are more respectful of alternative positions and more willing to consider them to be plausible or legitimate. An important result of seeing a political conflict as legitimate is a "greater willingness to extend civil liberties to even those groups whose political views one dislikes a great deal."[42]

Second, mixing increases the likelihood that people will be aware of competing rationales and see that their own arguments might be met by plausible counterarguments.[43] This effect is especially pronounced for those who antecedently show a "civil orientation toward conflict," in the sense that they are committed to a degree of social harmony and are willing to acknowledge, in advance, that dissenting views should be expressed.[44] These desirable effects of deliberation within mixed groups will not be realized in any deliberative process in which people are sorted, or sort themselves, into politically homogeneous groups.

There is a valuable lesson about possible uses of communications technologies to produce convergence, and possibly even learning, among people who disagree with one another. If people hear a wide range of arguments, they are more likely to be moved in the direction of those who disagree with them, at least if the arguments are reasonable and if those who disagree cannot easily be dismissed as untrustworthy or unreliable.

Cascades

The phenomenon of group polarization is closely related to the widespread phenomenon of "social cascades." No discussion of social fragmentation and emerging communications technologies would be complete without an understanding of cascades—above all because they become more likely when information, including false information, can be spread to hundreds, thousands, or even millions by the simple press of a button.

It is obvious that many social groups, both large and small, move rapidly and dramatically in the direction of one or another set of beliefs or actions.[45] These sorts of "cascades" typically involve the spread of information; in fact they are usually driven by information. Most of us lack direct or entirely reliable information about many matters of importance—whether global warming is a serious problem, whether there is a risk of war in India, whether al Qaeda is very dangerous, whether a lot of sugar is actually bad for you, whether Mars really exists, whether Pluto is a planet. If you lack a great deal of private information, you might well rely on the statements or actions of others.

To understand the dynamics here, we need to distinguish between two kinds of cascades: informational and reputational. In an informational cascade, people cease relying, at a certain point, on their private information or opinions. They decide instead on the basis of the signals conveyed by others. It follows that the behavior of the first few people can, in theory, produce similar behavior from countless followers. A stylized example: Suppose that Joan is unsure whether hybrid vehicles are in fact good for the environment; she may be moved in the direction of enthusiasm if Mary thinks that hybrid vehicles are good for the environment. If Joan and Mary are both favorably disposed toward hybrid vehicles, Carl may end up agreeing with them, at least if he lacks reliable independent information to the contrary. If Joan, Mary, and Carl believe that hybrid vehicles have large benefits, Don will have to have a good deal of confidence to reject their shared conclusion. And if Joan, Mary, Carl, and Don present a united front on the issue, others may well go along.

The example shows how information travels and can become quite widespread and entrenched, whether or not it is right. An illustration is the widespread popular belief that abandoned hazardous waste dumps rank among the most serious environmental problems; science does not support that belief, which seems to have spread via cascade.[46] Some cascades are widespread but local; consider the view, at one point with real currency in some African American communities, that white doctors are responsible for the spread of AIDS among African Americans. One group may end up believing something and another group the exact opposite, and the reason is the rapid transmission of information within one group but not the other.

Even among specialists and indeed doctors, cascades are common. "Most doctors are not at the cutting edge of research; their inevitable reliance upon what colleagues have done and are doing leads to numerous surgical fads and treatment-caused illnesses."[47] Thus an article in the influential *New England Journal of Medicine* explores "bandwagon diseases" in which doctors act like "lemmings, episodically and with a blind infectious enthusiasm pushing certain diseases and treatments primarily because everyone else is doing the same."[48] It should be easy to see how cascades might develop among groups of citizens. And when informational cascades are operating, there is a serious social problem: People who are in the cascade do not disclose, to their successors and to the public, the information that they privately hold.

We can imagine the possibility of *reputational cascades*, parallel to their informational siblings.[49] In a reputational cascade, people think that they know what is right, or what is likely to be right, but they nonetheless go along with the crowd in order to maintain the good opinion of others. Even the most confident people sometimes fall prey to this pressure, silencing themselves in the process. Fearing the wrath of others, people might not publicly contest practices and values that they privately abhor. The social practice of sexual harassment long predated the legal notion of "sexual harassment," and the innumerable women who were subject to harassment did not like it. But mostly they were silent, simply because they feared the consequences of public complaint. It is interesting to wonder how many current practices fall in the same

85

general category: they produce harm, and are known to produce harm, but they persist because most of those who are harmed believe that they will suffer if they object in public.

To see how a reputational cascade might work, suppose that Albert suggests that global warming is a serious problem, and that Barbara concurs with Albert, not because she actually thinks that Albert is right, but because she does not wish to seem, to Albert, to be ignorant or indifferent to environmental protection. If Albert and Barbara seem to agree that global warming is a serious problem, Cynthia might not contradict them publicly and might even appear to share their judgment, not because she believes that judgment to be correct, but because she does not want to face their hostility or lose their good opinion. It is easy to see how this process might generate a reputational cascade. Once Albert, Barbara, and Cynthia offer a united front on the issue, their friend David might be most reluctant to contradict them even if he thinks that they are wrong. The apparent views of Albert, Barbara, and Cynthia carry information; that apparent view might be right. But even if David thinks that they are wrong and has information supporting that conclusion, he might be most reluctant to take them on publicly.

Cybercascades: Information as Wildfire and Tipping Points

The Internet greatly increases the likelihood of diverse but inconsistent cascades. Cybercascades occur every day. Here is some fun and illuminating evidence from the domain of music.[50] Experimenters created an artificial music market, including 14,341 participants. The participants were given a list of previously unknown songs from unknown bands; they

were asked to listen to a brief selection of any songs that interested them, to decide what songs (if any) to download, and
to assign a rating to the songs they chose. About half of the
participants were asked to make their decisions independently, based on the names of the bands and the songs and
their own judgment about the quality of the music. About half
of the participants could see how many times each song had
been downloaded by other participants. These participants
were also randomly assigned to one or another of eight possible "worlds," with each evolving on its own; those in any particular world could see only the downloads in their own world.
A key question was whether people would be affected by the
choices of others—and whether different music would become popular in the different "worlds."

Did social influences matter? Did cascades develop? There
is not the slightest doubt. In all eight worlds, individuals are
more likely to download songs that had been previously downloaded in significant numbers, and less likely to download
songs that had not been so popular. Most strikingly, the success of songs is unpredictable; most songs can become very
popular or very unpopular, with much depending on the
choices of the first downloaders. The identical song can be a
hit or a failure, simply because other people, at the start, were
seen to choose to download it or not. To be sure, there is some
relationship between quality and success. "In general, the
'best' songs never do very badly, and the 'worst' songs never
do extremely well, but almost any other result is possible."
And in terms of their market shares, the best songs turn out
to be the most unpredictable of all! They can do exceptionally
well and also pretty badly, depending on whether social influences—the previous choices of others—suggest that they are
worth downloading.

87

The authors acknowledge that in many ways, the real world is different from this experiment. Media attention, marketing efforts, critical reviews, and other pressures may diminish the role of social influence. But such influence nevertheless plays a significant role and produces cascadelike results. When experts fail to predict success, it is "because when individual decisions are subject to social influence, markets do not simply aggregate pre-existing individual preferences." Note here that marketers often try hard to create early "buzz," by suggesting that a certain cultural product is already very popular; indeed, some marketing efforts actually involve artificial efforts to overstate the demand for the product, through purchases not by ordinary people, but by those allied with the artist. And if this is true for music, it is likely to be true for many other things as well, including movies, books, political candidates, and even ideas. ("Everyone is flocking to candidate X" or "idea Y is really catching on.") Candidates and ideas may enjoy stunning success (or failure), simply because social dynamics give them an early boost (or not). Here we can see a large effect from collaborative filtering, which may help create, and not merely reflect, individual preferences.

On the Internet, rumors often spread rapidly, and sometimes cascades are involved. Many of us have been deluged with email about the need to contact our representatives about some bill or other—only to learn that the bill did not exist and the whole problem was a joke or a fraud. Even more of us have been earnestly warned about the need to take precautions against viruses that do not exist. In the 1990s, many thousands of hours of Internet time were spent on elaborating paranoid claims about alleged nefarious activities, including murder, on the part of President Bill Clinton. A number of sites and discussion groups spread rumors and conspiracy theories of various sorts. "Electrified by the Internet, suspi-

88

cions about the crash of TWA Flight 800 were almost in-
stantly transmuted into convictions that it was the result of
friendly fire. . . . It was all linked to Whitewater. . . . Ideas
become E-mail to be duplicated and duplicated again."[51]

In 2000, an email rumor specifically targeted at African
Americans alleged that "No Fear" bumper stickers bearing
the logo of the sportswear company of the same name really
promote a racist organization headed by former Ku Klux Klan
Grand Wizard David Duke. Both terrorism and voting behavior have been prime areas for false rumors and occasional
cascade effects. In 2002, a widely circulated email said that
the Pentagon had not, in fact, been hit by a Boeing aircraft on
September 11. In 2004, many people were duly informed that
electronic voting machines had been hacked, producing massive fraud. (If you're interested in more examples, you might
consult http://snopes.com, a website dedicated to widely disseminated falsehoods, many of them spread via the Internet.)

Most of these examples are innocuous, because any cascade was rapidly corrected. But as a far more disturbing example, consider widespread doubts in South Africa about the
connection between HIV and AIDS. Any such doubts are especially troublesome, because a significant percentage of the
adult population is infected by the AIDS virus. South African
President Thabo Mbeki is a well-known Internet surfer, and
he learned the views of the "denialists" after stumbling across
one of their websites. The views of the denialists are not sci-
entifically respectable—but to a nonspecialist, many of the
claims on their (many) sites seem quite plausible. At least for
a period, President Mbeki both fell victim to a cybercascade
and, through his public statements, helped to accelerate
one—to the point where many South Africans at serious risk
were not convinced of an association between HIV and AIDS.

It is likely that this cascade effect produced a number of unnecessary infections and deaths.

With respect to information in general, there is even a "tipping point" phenomenon, creating a potential for dramatic shifts in opinion. After being presented with new information, people typically have different "thresholds" for choosing to believe or do something new or different. As the more likely believers—that is, people with low thresholds—come to a certain belief or action, people with somewhat higher thresholds then join them, soon producing a significant group in favor of the view in question. At that point, those with still higher thresholds may join, possibly to a point where a critical mass is reached, making large groups, societies, or even nations "tip."[52] The result of this process can be to produce snowball or cascade effects, as large groups of people end up believing something—whether or not that something is true or false—simply because other people in the relevant community seem to believe that it is true.

There is a great deal of experimental evidence of informational cascades, which are easy to induce in the laboratory;[53] real-world phenomena also have a great deal to do with cascade effects. Consider, for example, going to college, smoking, participating in political protests, voting for third-party candidates, striking, recycling, filing lawsuits, using birth control, rioting, even leaving bad dinner parties.[54] In all of these cases, people are greatly influenced by what others do. Often a tipping point will be reached. Sometimes we give an aura of inevitability to social developments, with the thought that deep cultural forces have led to (for example) an increase in smoking or protesting or a candidate's success, when in fact social influences have produces an outcome that could easily have been avoided. The Internet is an obvious breeding ground for cascades, and as a result, thousands or even millions of people who consult sources of a particular kind will move in one or another direction or even believe something that is quite false.

The good news is that the Internet is easily enlisted to debunk false rumors as well as to start them. For this reason, most such rumors do no harm. But it remains true that the opportunity to spread apparently credible information to so many people can induce fear, error, and confusion in a way that threatens many social goals, including democratic ones. As we have seen, this danger takes on a particular form in a balkanized speech market, as local cascades lead people in dramatically different directions. When this happens, correctives, even via the Internet, may work too slowly or not at all, simply because people are not listening to one another.

A Contrast: The Deliberative Opinion Poll

By way of contrast to polarization and cybercascades, consider some work by James Fishkin, a creative political scientist at Stanford University, who has pioneered a genuine social innovation: the deliberative opinion poll.[55] The basic idea is to ensure that polls are not mere "snapshots" of public opinion. Instead people's views are recorded only after diverse citizens, with different points of view, have actually been brought together in order to discuss topics with one another. Deliberative opinion polls have now been conducted in several nations, including the United States, England, and Australia. It is even possible for deliberative opinion polls to be conducted on the Internet, and Fishkin has initiated illuminating experiments in this direction.

In deliberative opinion polls, Fishkin finds some noteworthy shifts in individual views. But he does not find a systematic tendency toward polarization. (For a superbly helpful overview, see the Center for Deliberative Democracy website, http://cdd.stanford.edu/polls/docs/summary/.) In England, for example, deliberation led to reduced interest in using imprisonment as a tool for combating crime.[56] The percentage believing that "sending more offenders to prison" is an effective way to prevent crime fell from 57 to 38 percent; the percentage believing that fewer people should be sent to prison increased from 29 to 44 percent; belief in the effectiveness of "stiffer sentences" was reduced from 78 to 65 percent.[57] Similar shifts were shown in the direction of greater enthusiasm for procedural rights of defendants and increased willingness to explore alternatives to prison.

In other experiments with the deliberative opinion poll, shifts included a mixture of findings, with deliberation leading larger percentages of people to conclude that legal pressures should be increased on fathers for child support (from 70 to 85 percent) and that welfare and health care should be turned over to the states (from 56 to 66 percent).[58] These findings are consistent with the prediction of group polarization; and to be sure, the effect of deliberation was sometimes to create an increase in the intensity with which people held their preexisting convictions.[59] But this was hardly a uniform pattern. On some questions deliberation shifted a minority position to a majority position (with, for example, a jump from 36 to 57 percent of people favoring policies making divorce "harder to get"),[60] and it follows that sometimes majorities became minorities.

Fishkin's experiments have some distinctive features. They involve not like-minded people, but diverse groups of citizens engaged in discussion after being presented, by appointed moderators, with various sides of social issues. Fishkin's deliberators do not seek to obtain a group consensus; they listen and exchange ideas without being asked to come into agreement. In many ways these discussions provide a model for civic deliberation, complete with reason giving and political equality. Of course it can be expensive to transport diverse people to the same place. But new communications technologies make the idea of a deliberative opinion poll, and of reasoned discussion among heterogeneous people, far more feasible—even if private individuals, in their private capacity, would rarely choose to create deliberating institutions on their own. I have mentioned that Fishkin has created deliberative opinion polls on the Internet; there are many efforts and experiments in this general vein.[61]

Here we can find considerable promise for the future, in the form of discussions among diverse people who exchange reasons and who would not, without new technologies, be able to talk with one another at all. If we are guided by the notion of consumer sovereignty, and if we celebrate unlimited filtering, we will be unable to see why the discussions in the deliberative opinion poll are a great improvement over much of what is now happening on the Internet. In short, republican aspirations sharply diverge from the ideal of consumer sovereignty, through which we dream of a future in which, in Gates's words, "you'll be able to just say what you're interested in, and have the screen help you pick out a video that you care about."

The real questions are what sort of ideals we want to animate our choices, and what kinds of attitudes and regulation we want in light of that judgment. And here it is important to emphasize that in themselves, new technologies are not biased in favor of homogeneity and deliberation among like-minded people. Everything depends on what people seek to do with the new opportunities that they have. "I've been in chat rooms where I've observed, for the first time in my life,

93

African-Americans and white supremacists talking to each other. . . . [I]f you go through the threads of the conversation, by the end you'll find there's less animosity than there was at the beginning. It's not pretty sometimes . . . [b]ut here they are online, actually talking to each other."[62] The problem is that this is far from a universal practice.

Of Dangers and Solutions

I hope that I have shown enough to demonstrate that for citizens of a heterogeneous democracy, a fragmented communications market creates a considerable number of dangers. There are dangers for each of us as individuals; constant exposure to one set of views is likely to lead to errors and confusions, sometimes as a result of cybercascades. And to the extent that the process entrenches existing views, spreads falsehood, promotes extremism, and makes people less able to work cooperatively on shared problems, there are dangers for society as a whole.

To emphasize these dangers, it is unnecessary to claim that people do or will receive all of their information from the Internet. There are many sources of information, and some of them will undoubtedly counteract the risks I have discussed. Nor is it necessary to predict that most people are speaking only with those who are like-minded. Of course many people seek out or otherwise encounter competing views. But when technology makes it easy for people to wall themselves off from others, there are serious risks, for the people involved and for society generally.

Let me now disclose a central inspiration for this book, one that might seem far afield: *The Death and Life of Great American Cities*, by Jane Jacobs.[63] Among many other things, Jacobs offers an elaborate tribute to the sheer diversity of cities—to public spaces in which visitors encounter a range of people and practices that they could have barely imagined and that they could not possibly have chosen in advance. As Jacobs describes great cities, they teem and pulsate with life. "It is possible to be on excellent sidewalk terms with people who are very different from oneself and even, as time passes, on familiar public terms with them. Such relationships can, and do, endure for many years, for decades. . . . The tolerance, the room for great differences among neighbors—differences that often go far deeper than differences in color—which are possible and normal in intensely urban life . . . are possible and normal only when streets of great cities have built-in equipment allowing strangers to dwell in peace together. . . . Lowly, unpurposeful and random as they may appear, sidewalk contacts are the small change from which a city's wealth of public life may grow."[64]

Jacobs's book is about architecture, not communications. But with extraordinary vividness, Jacobs helps show, through an examination of city architecture, why we should be concerned about a situation in which people are able to create communications universes of their own liking. Jacobs's "sidewalk contacts" need not occur only on sidewalks. The idea of "architecture" should be taken broadly, not narrowly. And acknowledging the benefits that Jacobs finds on sidewalks, we might seek to find those benefits in many other places. At its best, I believe, a system of communications can be, for many of us, a close cousin or counterpart to a great urban center (while also being a lot safer, more convenient, and quieter). For a healthy democracy, shared public spaces, virtual or not, are a lot better than echo chambers.

To be sure, we do not yet know whether anything can or should be done about fragmentation and excessive self-insulation. I will take up that topic in due course. For purposes of obtaining understanding, few things are more important than to separate the question of whether there is a problem from the question of whether anything should be done about it. Dangers that cannot be alleviated continue to be dangers. They do not go away if or because we cannot, now or ever, think of decent solutions. It is much easier to think clearly when we appreciate that fact.

4

Social Glue and
Spreading Information

SOME PEOPLE believe that freedom of speech is a luxury. In their view, poor nations, or nations struggling with social and economic problems, should be trying not to promote democracy, but to ensure material well-being—economic growth, and a chance for everyone to have food, clothing, and shelter. This view is badly misconceived. If we understand what is wrong with it, we will have a much better sense of the social role of communications.

For many countries, the most devastating problem of all consists of famines, defined as widespread denial of access to food and, as a result, mass starvation. In the China famine of the late 1950s, for example, about 30 million people died. Is free speech a luxury for nations concerned about famine prevention? Would it be better for such nations to give a high priority, not to democracy and free speech, but to ensuring economic development? Actually these are foolish questions. Consider the astonishing finding, by the economist Amartya Sen, that in the history of the world, there has *never* been a famine in a system with a democratic press and free elections.[1] Sen's starting point here, which he also demonstrates empirically, is that famines are a social product, not an inevitable product of scarcity of food. Whether there will be a famine, as opposed to a mere shortage, depends on people's "entitlements," that is, what they are able to get. Even when food is limited, entitlements can be allocated in such a way as to ensure that no one will starve.

But when will a government take the necessary steps to prevent starvation? The answer depends on that government's own incentives. When there is a democratic system with free speech and a free press, the government faces a great deal of pressure to ensure that people generally have access to food. And where officials are thus pressured, they respond. But a system without a democratic press or free elections is likely to enable government to escape public retribution and hence not to respond to famines. Government officials will not be exposed, nor will they be at risk of losing their jobs.

Here, then, is a large lesson about the relationship between a well-functioning system of free expression and citizens' well-being. Free speech and free press are not mere luxuries or tastes of the most educated classes; they increase the likelihood that government will actually be serving people's interests. This lesson suggests some of the virtues, not only for liberty but also for economic development, of having freedom of speech.[2] And this lesson suggests the immense importance, for liberty and well-being, of the Internet itself, which makes it possible for countless people to learn about social and economic problems and to ask their governments to respond to what they have learned. It is no accident that tyrannical governments have tried to control access to the Internet, partly in order to wall citizens off from knowledge of other systems, partly to insulate their leaders from scrutiny and criticism. Knowledge is the great ally of both freedom and welfare.

But what may be most interesting for present purposes is the fact that once some people have the relevant knowledge—

a famine is actually on the horizon—they confer benefits, in the famine case massive benefits, on others who entirely lack that knowledge. Here cascades can be extremely desirable, and in a well-functioning democracy, the factual reports that actually "stick" turn out to be true. There can be no doubt that many of the people who are protected from starvation and death, as a result of this process, do not themselves choose in advance to learn about famines and related government policies. Many of the beneficiaries of democracy take little if any direct advantage of free media outlets or of democratic elections. But it is not necessary that they do so in order for the system to work. When some people know about the coming shortages, they can speak out. The consequence is that famines are averted. And what is true for famines is true for many other problems; natural disasters, including hurricanes and earthquakes, can be far less devastating if freedom is genuinely protected, simply because freedom can increase accountability. In the United States, the massive harm done in New Orleans by Hurricane Katrina was, in part, a failure of the democratic system, and it is profoundly to be hoped that democratic accountability will make such failures less likely in the future.

Shared Experiences

Thus far I have focused on the social problems that would result from a fragmented communications universe. Let us now turn to two related points. The first involves the social benefits of a situation in which many people, in a heterogeneous nation, have a number of common experiences. The second involves the fact that once one person has information, it tends to spread and hence to benefit others. A well-

functioning system of free expression is difficult to understand without reference to these points.

Many private and public benefits come from shared experiences and knowledge and also from a sense of shared tasks.
People are well aware of this, and they act accordingly. People
may watch what they watch, or do what they do, largely because other people are watching or doing the same thing. But
when the number of communications options grows dramatically, people will naturally make increasingly diverse choices,
and their shared experiences, plentiful in a time of general-
interest intermediaries, will decrease accordingly. This can
erode the kind of social glue that is provided by shared experience, knowledge, and tasks.

Consider in this regard an instructive discussion of Israel's
one-channel policy— ensuring, for a long period, that television "controlled by the Broadcasting Authority was the only
show in town."[3] From the standpoint of democracy, any such
policy obviously seems troublesome, indeed unacceptable. A
free society does not have a one-channel policy. But what is
less obvious, and more interesting, is some unintended consequences of that policy: Within two years of its inauguration,
"almost everybody watched almost everything on the one monopolistic channel. . . . Moreover, the shared experience of
viewing often made for conversation across ideological lines.
. . . [T]he shared central space of television news and public
affairs constituted a virtual town meeting." One lesson is that
a democracy "may be enhanced, rather than impeded, by
gathering its citizens in a single public space set aside for receiving and discussing reliable reports on the issues of the
day." It is not necessary to think that a one-channel policy is
good, or even tolerable, in order to recognize that shared viewing, providing common experiences for most or all people, can
be extremely valuable from the democratic point of view.

There is a connected point. Information has a special property: when any one of us learns something, other people, and perhaps many other people, are likely to benefit from what we have learned. If you find out about crime in the neighborhood, or about risks associated with certain foods, others will gain from that knowledge. In a system with general-interest intermediaries, many of us come across information from which we may not substantially benefit as individuals, but which we spread to others. Society as a whole is much better off as a result. As we will see, a system in which individuals can design their own communications universe threatens to undermine this salutary process, not only because of the risk of spreading false information via cybercascades, but also because the situation of fragmentation prevents true information from spreading as much as it should.

Solidarity Goods

Most people understand the importance of common experiences, and many of our practices reflect a firm sense of the point. National holidays, for example, help constitute a nation, by encouraging citizens to think, all at once, about events of shared importance. And they do much more than this. They enable people, in all their diversity, to have some common memories and concerns.

At least this is true in nations where national holidays have a vivid and concrete meaning, as they do, for example, in younger democracies such as South Africa, India, and Israel. In the United States, many national holidays have become mere days-off-from-work, and the precipitating occasion for the day off—President's Day, Memorial Day, Labor Day—has come to be nearly invisible; we seem to have forgotten our

101

history, the struggles and celebrations that gave rise to the holidays themselves. This is a serious loss. With the partial exception of July 4th, Martin Luther King Jr. Day is probably the closest thing to a genuinely substantive national holiday, largely because that celebration involves recent events that can be treated as concrete and meaningful. In other words, the holiday is *about* something. A shared celebration of a holiday with a clear meaning helps to constitute a nation and to bring diverse citizens together.

Nor need such events be limited to nations. Recall, as an especially dramatic example, the shared worldwide celebration of the Millennium, welcomed in sequence by India, China, Egypt, France, England, New York, Chicago, and California. In a similar vein, one of the great values of the Olympics is its international quality, allowing people from different countries to form bounds of commonality, both directly through participation by athletes and indirectly through shared viewing and interest. Of course the Olympics is also a vehicle for crude forms of nationalism. But at its best, the governing ethos is cosmopolitan in spirit.

Communications and the media are of course exceptionally important here. Sometimes millions of people follow an election, a sports event, or the coronation of a new monarch; and many of them do so because of the simultaneous actions of others. In this sense, some of the experiences made possible by modern technologies are *solidarity goods*, in the sense that their value goes up when and because many other people are enjoying or consuming them. The point very much bears on the historic role of both public forums and general-interest intermediaries. Street corners and public parks were and remain places where diverse people can congregate and see one another. General-interest intermediaries, if they are operating properly, give many people, all at once, a clear sense of social problems and tasks.

Why might these shared experiences be so desirable or important? There are three principal reasons.

- Simple enjoyment may not be the most important thing, but it is far from irrelevant. Often people like many experiences—including experiences associated with television, radio, and the Internet—simply because those experiences are being shared. Consider a popular movie, the Super Bowl, or a presidential debate. For many of us, these are goods that are worth less, and possibly worthless, if many others are not enjoying or purchasing them too. Hence a presidential debate may be worthy of individual attention, for many people, in part because so many other people consider it worthy of individual attention.

- Sometimes shared experiences help to promote and to ease social interactions, permitting people to speak with one another, and to congregate around a common issue, task, or concern, whether or not they have much in common. In this sense shared experiences provide a form of social glue. They help make it possible for diverse people to believe that they live in the same culture. Indeed they help constitute that shared culture, simply by creating common memories and experiences, and a sense of a common enterprise.

- A fortunate consequence of shared experiences—and in particular many of those produced by general-interest intermediaries—is that people who would otherwise see one another as quite unfamiliar, in extreme cases as nearly belonging to a different species, can come instead to regard one another as fellow citizens

103

with shared hopes, goals, and concerns. This is a subjective good—felt and perceived as a good—for those directly involved. But it can be an objective good as well, especially if it leads to cooperative projects of various kinds. When people learn about a disaster faced by fellow citizens, for example, they may respond with financial and other help. In the aftermath of the attacks of 9/11, Americans did exactly that, and saw one another, to a greater and deeper extent, as involved in a common enterprise. The point applies internationally as well as domestically; massive relief efforts are often made possible by virtue of the fact that millions of people learn, all at once, about the relevant need.

Any well-functioning society depends on relationships of trust and reciprocity, in which people see their fellow citizens as potential allies, willing to help and deserving of help when help is needed. The level, or stock, of these relationships sometimes goes by the name of "social capital."[4] We might generalize the points made thus far by suggesting that shared experiences, emphatically including those made possible by the system of communications, contribute to desirable relationships among citizens, even strangers. A society without such experiences will inevitably suffer a decline in those relationships.

Fewer Shared Experiences

Even in a nation of unlimited communications options, some events will inevitably attract widespread attention. On the Internet itself, some sites play an especially prominent role; a degree of centralization remains. But simply as a matter of numbers, an increasingly diverse communications universe will reduce the level of shared experiences. When there were only three television networks, much of what appeared on television would have the quality of a genuinely common experience. The lead story on the evening news would provide the same reference point for many millions of people. This is decreasingly true. In recent decades, the three major networks have lost tens of millions of viewers. As a result of increased options, the most highly rated show on current network television has far fewer viewers than the fifteenth most highly rated show in a typical year in the 1970s.

To the extent that choices and filtering proliferate, it is inevitable that diverse individuals, and diverse groups, will share fewer reference points. Events that are highly salient to some people will barely register on others' viewscreens. And it is possible that some views and perspectives that seem obvious for many people will, for others, be barely intelligible.

This is far from an unambiguously bad thing. On balance, it is almost certainly good. When people are able to make specific choices, they are likely to enjoy what they are seeing or doing. Of course a degree of diversity, with respect to both topics and points of view, is highly desirable. I am hardly suggesting that everyone should be required to watch the same thing. The question does not involve requirements at all. My only claim is that a common set of frameworks and experiences is valuable for a heterogeneous society, and that a system with limitless options, making for diverse choices, will compromise some important social values. If we think, with Justice Brandeis, that a great menace to freedom is an "inert people," and if we believe that a set of common experiences promotes active citizenship and mutual self-understanding, we will be concerned by any developments that greatly reduce those experiences. The ideal of consumer sovereignty makes it hard even to understand this concern. But from the standpoint of republican ideals, the concern should lie at the center of any evaluation of the system of communications.

What Consumers Might Do and What Producers Might Do

None of this means that shared experiences are disappearing. Of course people know that such experiences are desirable, and often they cooperate with one another so as to ensure that they will have such experiences. Of course the Internet and email make communication much easier, so that like-minded people can decide, at once, to do or watch the same thing. Collaborative filtering can be effective here. If you know that most "people like you" are going to go see a new movie starring Brad Pitt, you might be more likely to go see that movie. Consumers themselves can band together, across geographical lines, to ensure that they do or watch the same thing. In this way new communications technologies can actually promote shared experiences, even among people who do not know each other or who would not otherwise think of one another as group members. But even with email, collaborative filtering, and discussion groups, it can be harder for large numbers of people to coordinate around a single option, at least when the array of options is itself extremely large. This point is enough to suggest the basis for my general concern.

Producers of information also have strong incentives to get people to coordinate around a shared option. They might themselves emphasize, for example, that most people, or most people like you, will be watching a television show dealing with crime in the area, or with the difficulty of raising children in an urban environment. Or advertisers might stress the importance, for diverse people, of examining a certain website, in general or at a specific time. In fact an extremely effective way of getting people to engage in certain conduct is to say that most people, or most people like you, are doing exactly that. In this way, ordinary market forces are likely to diminish the problem.

But they will not eliminate it. To the extent that options are limitless, it is inevitable that producers will have some difficulty in getting people to watch something together, even if people would benefit from this activity. It is more likely that diverse groups, defined in demographic, political, or other terms, will occasionally coordinate on agreed-upon alternatives; and this will introduce the various problems associated with fragmentation and group polarization.

Information as a Public Good

Thus far I have dealt with the purposes served by ensuring common experiences, many of them made available via the media. There is a related and equally important point. Information is a "public good" in a technical sense used by economists: when one person knows something, others are likely to be benefited as well. If you learn that a heat wave is coming, or that there is a high risk of criminal assault three blocks away, other people are highly likely to learn these things too. In the terminology of economics, those of us who learn things do not fully "internalize" the benefits of that learning; the benefits amount to "positive externalities" for other people.

In this respect, information has properties in common with environmental protection and national defense. When one person is helped by a program for cleaner air, or by a strong military, other people will necessarily be helped as well. It is standard to say that in circumstances of this kind—when public goods are involved—it is hazardous to rely entirely on individual choices. Acting on their own, those who litter or otherwise pollute are all too likely not to consider the harms they impose on others. Acting on their own, people are all too likely not to contribute to national defense, hoping that others will pick up the slack.

What is true for pollution and national defense is true as well for information. Made solely with reference to the concerns of the individuals involved, private choices will produce too much pollution and too little in the way of national defense or information. When you learn, or do not learn, about the pattern of crime in your city or about whether climate change is a serious problem, you are usually unlikely to be thinking about the consequences of your learning, or failure to learn, for other people (except perhaps your immediate family). An implication is that an individual's rational choices, made only with reference to individual self-interest, will produce too little knowledge of public affairs. These are the most conventional cases of "market failure"—addressed, in the context of pollution and national defense, by government programs designed to overcome the predictable problems that would come from relying entirely on individual choices.

No one ever planned this, but if they are working well, general-interest intermediaries provide an excellent corrective here. When individuals do not design their communications universe on their own, they will be exposed to a great deal of material from which they may not much benefit as individuals, but from which they will be able to help many others. Perhaps you would not ordinarily seek out material about new asthma treatments for children; but once you learn a little bit about them, you might tell your friends whose son has asthma. Perhaps you are not much interested in environmental risks; but once you learn about hazards associated with sports utility vehicles, you might be reinforced in your desire not to buy one, and you might tell people you know about the underlying problems, trying to convince them. Every day, in fact, millions of people are beneficiaries of information that they receive only because someone else who has not sought out that information in advance happens to learn it.

This is emphatically not an argument that from the point of view of dissemination of information, it would be better to abolish the Internet and to rely on a system dominated by a few general-interest intermediaries. Nothing could be further from the truth. As we have seen, new technologies dramatically accelerate the spreading of information, true as well as false. General-interest intermediaries have interests and biases of their own, and for sheer practical reasons, they cannot provide exposure to all topics and viewpoints. On balance, the increase in options is likely to produce more and better information. My only suggestion is that insofar as there is a perfect ability to filter, people will sometimes fail to learn things from which they might have ended up benefiting others. Even if an increase in communications options is, with respect to information, a significant gain, this remains a serious loss.

Famine as Metaphor, and a Clarification

Return now to Amartya Sen's finding that famines do not occur in nations with free elections and a democratic press. We should take all this not as an isolated or exotic example limited to poor countries at risk of famine, but as a metaphor for countless situations in which a democratic government averts social problems precisely because political pressure forces it do so. The underlying problems often involve crime, pollution, natural disasters, employment opportunities, health risks, medical advances, political candidates, even corruption.

This point shows that there are serious problems if information is seen as an ordinary consumer product. The simple reason is that in a system in which individuals make choices among innumerable options based only on their private interest, they will fail to learn about topics and views from which they may not much benefit, but from which others would gain a great deal.

The new technology has great potential on these counts as well. If the press is free, and the Internet is available, information about a potential or actual famine, or any other problem, can be spread to an entire nation, even the entire world. Fragmentation might even help here, at least if relevant information spreads across the fragmented groups; the problem arises if such spreading does not occur. What I am offering is not a complaint about the Internet, but an account of the frequently overlooked importance, for a system of free expression, of shared experiences and the provision of information to people who would not have chosen it in advance.

Of Niches and Very Long Tails

In an illuminating and instructive book, Chris Anderson, the editor of *Wired*, celebrates niches and niche marketing, seeing them as an extraordinary development made possible by the Internet.[5] To make a complex story short, Anderson argues that companies can, and do, make increasing amounts of money by catering to niche markets through a large volume of products (books à la Amazon.com, movies à la Netflix).

Many of these products are bought by very few people. At a bookstore, very little money can be made by the poor sellers, which are at the end of the long tail of the distribution system. At Amazon.com, by contrast, the immense stock of books and the large customer base can ensure that significant aggregate sales come from the long tail.

Anderson sees this as an important and wonderful trend. With the aid of the Internet, and of other modern technologies, it is often nearly costless to sell not just the blockbusters, but also goods that cater to small markets. Indeed, the total profits from doing so may be very high. "Niche" is a key word in Anderson"s argument.

Anderson is right to emphasize that the Internet can greatly increase niche marketing, in a way that offers extraordinary economic opportunities from the long tail. He is also right to suggest that communities can form around highly specialized tastes. What is remarkable is his near-complete lack of self-consciousness about what might be wrong with a world of niches. Anderson writes as if the power to choose the particular good that each particular person particularly wants is an unambiguous good—as if there is little to do but to notice and celebrate this process. Anderson's analysis appears implicitly premised on the idea that freedom and the good life are promoted by, and maybe even captured in, the opportunity to choose what is specifically sought on either the large head or the long tail. Of course he is right to celebrate the increase in available options, but from the standpoint of democracy, the assessment is not so simple.

The refusal to raise questions about the proliferation of niches is characteristic of a great deal of thinking about the Internet, even among its most creative and sharpest analysts. Indeed, we might go further. Many of those who know most about the underlying technology and about what is becoming

possible often display a kind of visceral, unreflective libertari-
anism—a belief that all that matters is that people are allowed
to see what they want and to choose what they like. The commitments to free markets and to perfecting them are no less
intense than what can be found in the ideas of the Chicago
School of economics, most famously captured in the work of
Milton Friedman. As a long-time member of the University
of Chicago faculty, I confess a great deal of fondness for the
Chicago School; in my view, it is mostly right, and certainly
more right than wrong. For consumer goods—such as sneak-
ers, cars, soaps, and candy—it provides the right foundation
for analysis. But when we are speaking of politics and the
democratic domain, it misses a great deal.

What must be engaged is the risk that the proliferation of
niches will have adverse effects on aspects of the shared culture and also promote fragmentation, particularly along political lines. It is not enough to rest content with general obser-
vations about how many people are curious and how niches
include and even create shared cultures of different kinds.

Of Biases and Elites

It is an understatement to say that many people deplore the
mass media. Some insist that television networks and large
newspapers are biased in one direction or another. Others
think that they are hopelessly superficial, even sensationalistic, obsessed with crimes and celebrities and sound bites. Still
others think that general-interest intermediaries are inevitably few in number, and hence that they produce a stifling degree of homogeneity. For any of these people, a world with the
Internet is infinitely better than a world in which general-

interest intermediaries dominate the scene. In this light, any effort to celebrate those intermediaries and to emphasize the risks of social fragmentation might seem positively quaint at best. Isn't it elitist, or confused, to wish for a world in which people cannot read what they want and are subjected to filters by a self-appointed media elite?

I have not argued that it would be desirable for a few newspapers and broadcasters to dominate the scene. With the Internet, the situation is definitely better, not worse. Nor do I claim that newspapers and broadcasters generally do an excellent or even a good job. Those who think that newspapers and weekly magazines are biased or otherwise inadequate should have no quarrel with the suggestion that unchosen encounters and shared experiences, of one or another sort, are important for democracy.

Of course some of the most popular Internet sites work in a very similar fashion to general-interest intermediaries. Indeed, they *are* general-interest intermediaries, performing the same functions online that they perform on television or on paper; consider ABC, CBS, NBC, Fox News, the *New York Times*, the *Washington Post*, the *Los Angeles Times*, the *Wall Street Journal*, and many more. In any case, many popular sites contain links, advertising, and multiple news stories. To the extent that important Internet sites continue to serve the social role of intermediaries, there is less to worry about. But there is nonetheless a difference between an evening program or a newspaper, which set whole stories before your eyes, and an Internet site, which may contain a headline or a quick link to a new topic. It is true and important that the most popular sites contain links, advertising, and multiple news stories. But concerns about self-insulation nonetheless remain.

113

The Networked Public Sphere?

What do we actually know about use of the Internet? Not nearly enough. But a picture is emerging. In a careful and illuminating analysis, Yochai Benkler describes, and celebrates, the "networked public sphere."[6]

The idea of the Daily Me points to the risk of social fragmentation. But precisely because time is limited, it is possible to think that the Internet will not make much of a difference—that a few providers will dominate the Internet no less than they dominate television and radio. On the Internet, attention is a scarce commodity, and it is inevitable that many people will congregate around a few major sites, perhaps the sites of those that constitute the mass media in any case. The *New York Times* and the *Washington Post* have large circulations and millions of people visit their sites; the *New Republic* and the *National Review* have significant but much smaller circulations, and they are read online in similar proportions; the University of Chicago Law School Faculty Blog (wonderful and endlessly entertaining though it may be) is not likely to have millions of readers, even on its best days. If we emphasize these points, continuing concentration, rather than echo chambers, might seem to be the wave of the future.

But as Benkler shows, this prediction is inconsistent with the emerging reality. To be sure, some sites are exceedingly popular and others are seen by very few people. At the same time, the new model is very different from that of the old mass media. In Benkler's words, "clusters of moderately read sites provide platforms for vastly greater numbers of speakers than were heard in the mass-media environment."[7] Even if your site or your blog has very few readers, one of those readers might draw your words to the attention of someone with more readers. If that happens, a still more popular site might pick up your words, and eventually you might have a real influence. Something of this kind happens in the blogosphere every day, and it works for smaller websites as well. To be sure, the real Internet does not operate as a system in which "everyone is a pamphleteer." But it is very different from what preceded it, simply because it has so many more voices, so much more information, and such broader participation.

Like many others, Benkler insists that the networked public sphere is immune from the risks of fragmentation and polarization—that a common discourse remains, in the form of a public sphere that generates shared concerns and public knowledge. Benkler's interpretation is not exactly wrong, but his own evidence complicates his conclusion. As he suggests, we now know that "sites cluster—in particular, topically and interest-related sites link much more heavily to each other than to other sites."[8] Of course this has been precisely my concern here. In the same vein, careful evidence shows that in the blogosphere, liberals link to one another, and so too for conservatives (see chapter 6 for more details). Many people therefore segregate themselves along lines of both topics and point of view. In Benkler's own words, individuals "cluster around topical, organizational, or other common features,"[9] and like-minded people "read each other and quote each other much more than . . . the other side,"[10] if only to sort out their internal disagreements.

In 2004, a valuable study explored whether people are, in fact, using the Internet to screen out ideas with which they disagree.[11] The study concludes otherwise—that many Americans are learning about competing views, and receiving information that runs counter to their predilections. But here too, the underlying evidence is complicated. It is true that of those with a position on the two candidates for the presidency in the 2004 election—President Bush and Senator John Kerry— fully 43 percent were aware of arguments for and against both candidates. Another 21 percent were essentially tuned out, and were unaware of arguments relating to either candidate. Note, however, that 29 percent of people (nearly a third!) showed a kind of echo-chamber effect: they were well aware of the arguments in favor of their candidate but knew very little about the arguments in favor of the opposing candidate. In addition, about 25 percent of people candidly acknowledged that they prefer to get their news from sources that conform to their own views. If 25 percent of people acknowledged this point, the actual figure is almost certainly larger. (Recall that Republicans prefer Fox News, which Democrats try to avoid.)

It is true that in this study, the echo-chamber effect was not a more serious problem among Internet users than among those who do not use the Internet. On the contrary, people with high-speed home connections were somewhat more likely to know arguments on both sides. But this finding should not be surprising. Other things being equal, those with a high-speed home connection should be expected to be both more educated and more interested in politics. It is not exactly a shock to find that they are more likely to be aware of arguments for and against presidential candidates. But mere knowledge of those arguments is hardly a sufficient safeguard against the risk of fragmentation. You may know that some people think the opposing candidate is good; you may even have a sense of why they like him. But if you have learned all this in a way that casts ridicule and contempt on him and his supporters, you may not have learned much. (I will return to this point in connection with the blogosphere.)

Of course the Daily Me is not a lived reality. (The site by that name is a newspaper covering the state of Maine!) There remains a great deal of centralization on the Internet, if only because of the existence of especially popular sites; but Benkler is right to point to the existence of a networked public sphere. Facts and opinions on liberal sites often migrate to conservative sites, and vice versa. It is also true that even if opinions are clustering, society can ultimately benefit from the wide range of arguments that ultimately make their way to the general public. The current situation is hardly worse than what preceded it; on the contrary, it is much better, if only because of the increase in the number and range of voices. The question is not, however, whether the present is better than the past, but whether we can make the present and the future better still.

Spreading Information

A heterogeneous society benefits from shared experiences, many of them produced by the media. These shared experiences provide a kind of social glue, facilitating efforts to solve shared problems, encouraging people to view one another as fellow citizens, and sometimes helping to ensure responsiveness to genuine problems and needs, even helping to identify them as such. A special virtue of unsought exposures to information is that even if individuals frequently do not gain much from that information, they will tell other people about it, and it is here that the information will prove beneficial.

To the extent that the communications market becomes more personalized, it reduces the range of shared experiences and at the same time fails to confer some of the benefits

117

that come when individuals receive information, often more helpful to others than to themselves, that they would not have chosen in advance. If the role of public forums and general-interest intermediaries is diminished, and if good substitutes do not develop, those benefits will be diminished as well, with harmful results for republican ideals.

5

Citizens

THE AUTHORS of the American Constitution met behind closed doors in Philadelphia during the summer of 1787. When they completed their labors, the American public was, naturally enough, exceedingly curious about what they had done. A large crowd gathered around what is now known as Convention Hall. One of its members asked Benjamin Franklin, as he emerged from the building, "What have you given us?" Franklin's answer was hopeful, or perhaps a challenge: "A republic, if you can keep it." In fact we should see Franklin's remark as a reminder of a continuing obligation. The text of any founding document is likely to be far less important in maintaining a republic than the actions and commitments of the nation's citizenry over time.

This suggestion raises questions of its own. What is the relationship between our choices and our freedom? Between citizens and consumers? And how do the answers relate to the question of whether, and how, government should deal with people's emerging power to filter speech content?

In this chapter my basic claim is that we should evaluate new communications technologies, including the Internet, by asking how they affect us as citizens and not only by asking how they affect us as consumers. A central question is whether emerging social practices, including consumption patterns,

119

are promoting or compromising our own highest aspirations. More particularly I make two suggestions, designed to undermine from a new direction the idea that consumer sovereignty is the appropriate goal for communications policy.

The first is that people's preferences do not come from nature or from the sky. They are a product, at least in part, of social circumstances, including existing institutions, available options, social influences, and past choices. Prominent among the circumstances that create preferences are markets themselves. "Free marketeers have little to cheer about if all they can claim is that the market is efficient at filling desires that the market itself creates."[1] Unrestricted consumer choices are important, sometimes very important. But they do not exhaust the idea of freedom, and they should not be equated with it.

The second point has to do with the fact that in their capacity as citizens, people often seek policies and goals that diverge from the choices they make in their capacity as consumers. If citizens seek to do this, there is no legitimate objection from the standpoint of freedom—at least if citizens are not disfavoring any particular point of view or otherwise violating rights. Often citizens attempt to promote their highest aspirations through democratic institutions. If the result is to produce a communications market that is different from what individual consumers would seek—if as citizens we produce a market, for example, that promotes exposure to serious issues and a range of shared experiences—freedom will be promoted, not undermined.

The two points are best taken together. Citizens are often aware that they are subject to multiple influences and that their private choices, under a system of limitless options, may lead in unfortunate directions, both for them as individuals and for society at large. They might believe, for example, that their own choices, with respect to television and the Internet, do not entirely promote their own well-being, or that of society as a whole. They might attempt to restructure alternatives and institutions so as to improve the situation.

At the same time, I will suggest that even insofar as we are consumers, new purchasing opportunities, made ever more available through the Internet, are far less wonderful than we like to think. The reason is that these opportunities are accelerating the "consumption treadmill," in which we buy more and better goods, not because they make us happier or better off, but because they help us keep us with others. As citizens, we might well seek to slow down this treadmill, so as to ensure that social resources are devoted, not to keeping up with one another, but to goods and services that really improve our lives.

Choices and Circumstances: The Formation and Deformation of Preferences

Many people seem to think that freedom consists in respect for consumption choices, whatever their origins and content. Indeed, this thought appears to underlie enthusiasm for the principle of consumer sovereignty itself. On this view, the central goal of a well-functioning system of free expression is to ensure unrestricted choice. A similar conception of freedom underlies many of the celebrations of emerging communications markets.

It is obvious that a free society is generally respectful of people's choices. But freedom imposes certain preconditions, ensuring not just respect for choices and the satisfaction of preferences, whatever they happen to be, but also the free formation of desires and beliefs. Most preferences and beliefs

121

do not preexist social institutions; they are formed and shaped by existing arrangements. Much of the time, people develop tastes for what they are used to seeing and experiencing. If you are used to seeing stories about the local sports team, your interest in the local sports team is likely to increase. If news programming deals with a certain topic—say, welfare reform, environmental protection, or a current threat of war—your taste for that topic is likely to be strengthened. If you learn that most people like a certain movie, or book, or political candidate, or idea, you will be more likely to like them too; and this effect is increased if the relevant people are "like you." Recall the experiment with music downloads, in which the success or failure of songs was largely a product of people's perceptions of what other people had done.

When people are deprived of opportunities, they are likely to adapt and to develop preferences and tastes for what little they have. We are entitled to say that the deprivation of opportunities is a deprivation of freedom—even if people have adapted to it and do not much want anything more.

Similar points hold for the world of communications. If people are deprived of access to competing views on public issues, and if as a result they lack a taste for those views, they lack freedom, whatever the nature of their preferences and choices. If people are exposed mostly to sensationalistic coverage of the lives of movie stars, or only to sports, or only to left-of-center views, and never to international issues, their preferences will develop accordingly. If people are mostly watching a conservative station—say, Fox News—they will inevitably be affected by what they see. Whatever one's political view, there is, in an important respect, a problem from the standpoint of freedom itself. This is so even if people are voluntarily choosing the limited fare.

The general idea here—that preferences and beliefs are a product of existing institutions and practices, and that the result can be a form of unfreedom, one of the most serious of all—is hardly new. It is a longstanding theme in political and legal thought. Thus Tocqueville wrote of the effects of the institution of slavery on the desires of many slaves themselves: "Plunged in this abyss of wretchedness, the Negro hardly notices his ill fortune; he was reduced to slavery by violence, and the habit of servitude has given him the thoughts and ambitions of a slave; he admires his tyrants even more than he hates them and finds his joy and pride in servile imitation of his oppressors."[2] In the same vein, John Dewey wrote that "social conditions may restrict, distort, and almost prevent the development of individuality."[3] He insisted that we should therefore "take an active interest in the working of social institutions that have a bearing, positive or negative, upon the growth of individuals." For Dewey, a just society "is as much interested in the positive construction of favorable institutions, legal, political, and economic, as it is in the work of removing abuses and overt oppressions." Robert Frank and Philip Cook have urged that in the communications market, existing "financial incentives strongly favor sensational, lurid and formulaic offerings," and that the resulting structure of rewards "is especially troubling in light of evidence that, beginning in infancy and continuing through life, the things we see and read profoundly alter the kinds of people we become."[4]

Every tyrant knows that it is important, and sometimes possible, not only to constrain people's actions but also to manipulate their desires, partly by making people fearful, partly by putting certain options in an unfavorable light, partly by limiting information. And nontyrannical governments are hardly neutral with respect to preferences and desires. They hope to

123

have citizens who are active rather than passive, curious rather than indifferent, engaged rather than inert. Indeed, the basic institutions of private property and freedom of contract—fundamental to free societies and indeed to freedom of speech—have important effects on the development of preferences themselves. Thus both private property and freedom of contract have long been defended, not on the ground that they are neutral with respect to preferences, but on the ground that they help to form good preferences—by producing an entrepreneurial spirit and by encouraging people to see one another, not as potential enemies or as members of different ethnic groups, but as potential trading partners.[5] The right to free speech is itself best seen as part of the project of helping to produce an engaged, self-governing citizenry.

Limited Options: Of Foxes and Sour Grapes

When government imposes restrictions on people's opportunities and information, it is likely to undermine freedom not merely by affecting their choices but also by affecting their preferences and desires. Of course, this is what concerned Tocqueville and Dewey, and in unfree nations, we can find numerous examples in the area of communications and media policy, as official censorship prevents people from learning about a variety of ideas and possibilities. This was common practice in Communist nations in the Soviet bloc, and both China and Singapore have sought to reduce general access to the Internet, partly in an effort to shape both preferences and beliefs. When information is unavailable and when opportunities are shut off, and known to be shut off, people may not end up not wanting them at all.

124

The social theorist Jon Elster illustrates the point through the old tale of the fox and the sour grapes.[6] The fox does not want the grapes because he believes them to be sour; but the fox believes them to be sour because they are unavailable, and he adjusts his attitude toward the grapes in a way that takes account of their unavailability. The fox cannot have the grapes, and so he concludes that they are sour and that he doesn't want them. Elster says, quite rightly, that the unavailability of the grapes cannot be justified by reference to the preferences of the fox, when the unavailability of the grapes is the very *reason* for the preferences of the fox.

Elster's suggestion is that citizens who have been deprived of options may not want the things of which they have been deprived; and the deprivation cannot be justified by reference to the fact that citizens are not asking for these things, when they are not asking *because* they have been deprived of them. We can identify a problem with authoritarian systems in this light. Imagine that an authoritarian government ensures a system of few or dramatically limited options—including, for example, an official government news program, and nothing else. It is predictable that many citizens will despise that system, at least when they speak privately. But even if there is little or no public demand for more options, the system cannot reasonably be defended on the ground that most people do not object to it. The absence of the demand is likely to be a product of the deprivation. It does not justify the deprivation. This point holds with respect to television and radio stations as with everything else.

Thus far I have been making arguments for a range of opportunities, even in societies in which people, lacking such opportunities, are not asking for more. Of course the issue is very different in the communications universe that is the main topic of this book—one in which people have countless

125

possibilities from which to choose. But here too social circumstances, including markets, affect preferences, not only the other way around. From the standpoint of citizenship, and freedom as well, problems can emerge when people are choosing alternatives that sharply limit their own horizons.

Preferences are a product not only of the number of options but also of what markets accentuate, of social influences, and of past choices, and those choices can impose constraints of their own. Suppose, for example, that one person's choices have been limited to sports, and lead him to learn little about political issues; that another person focuses only on national issues because she has no interest in what happens outside American borders; and that still another restricts himself to material that reaffirms his own political convictions. In different ways, each of these persons' choices constrains both citizenship and freedom, simply because it dramatically narrows their field of interests and concerns. This is not a claim that people should be required to see things that do not interest them; it is a more mundane point about how any existing market and our own choices can limit or expand our freedom.

Indeed people are often aware of this fact and make choices so as to promote wider understanding and better formation of their own preferences. Sometimes we select radio and television programs, and Internet sites, from which we will learn something, even if the programs and the sites we choose are more challenging and less fun than the alternatives. And we may even lament the very choices that we make, on the ground that what we have done, as consumers, does not serve our long-term interests. Whether or not people actually lament their choices, they sometimes have good reason to do so, and they know this without admitting it.

These points underlie some of the most important functions of public forums and of general-interest intermediaries.

Both of these produce unanticipated exposures that help promote the free formation of preferences, even in a world of numerous options. In this sense, they are continuous with the educational system. Indeed they provide a kind of continuing education for adults, something that a free society cannot do without. It does not matter whether the government is directly responsible for the institutions that perform this role. What matters is that they exist.

Democratic Institutions and Consumer Sovereignty

None of these points means that some abstraction called "government" should feel free to move preferences and beliefs in what it considers to be desirable directions. The central question is whether citizens in a democratic system, aware of the points made thus far, might want to make choices that diverge from those that they make in their capacity as private consumers. Sometimes this does appear to be their desire. What I am suggesting is that when this is the case, there is, in general, no legitimate objection if government responds. The public's effort to counteract the adverse effects of consumer choices should not be disparaged as a form of government meddling or unacceptable paternalism, at least if the government is democratic, and reacting to the reflective judgments of the citizenry.

What we think and what we want often depends on the social role in which we find ourselves, and the role of citizen is very different from the role of consumer. Citizens do not think and act as consumers. Indeed, most citizens have no difficulty in distinguishing between the two roles. Frequently a nation's political choices could not be understood if viewed only as a process of implementing people's desires in their capacity as consumers. For example, some people support efforts to promote serious coverage of public issues on television, even though their own consumption patterns favor reality shows and situation comedies; they seek stringent laws protecting the environment or endangered species even though they do not use the public parks or derive material benefits from protection of such species; they approve of laws calling for social security and welfare even though they do not save or give to the poor; they support antidiscrimination laws even though their own behavior is hardly race- or gender-neutral. The choices people make as political participants seem systematically different from those they make as consumers.

Why is this? Is it a puzzle or a paradox? The most basic answer is that people's behavior as citizens reflects a variety of distinctive influences. In their role as citizens, people might seek to implement their highest aspirations when they do not do so in private consumption. They might aspire to a communications system of a particular kind, one that promotes democratic goals, and they might try to promote that aspiration through law. Acting in the fashion of Ulysses anticipating the sirens, people might "precommit" themselves, in democratic processes, to a course of action that they consider to be in the general interest. And in their capacity as citizens, they might attempt to satisfy altruistic or other-regarding desires, which diverge from the self-interested preferences often characteristic of the behavior of consumers in markets.

In fact social and cultural norms can incline people to express aspirational or altruistic goals more often in political behavior than in markets. Of course it is true that selfish behavior is common in politics; but social norms sometimes press people, in their capacity as citizens, in the direction of a concern for others or for the public interest. Acting together as citizens, people can solve collective-action problems that prove intractable for consumers. For each of us, acting individually, it is nearly impossible to make any substantial contribution to the problem of air pollution or to the assistance of those who are suffering from the effects of a natural disaster. But if we are able to act collectively—perhaps through private institutions, perhaps through government—we might be able to do a great deal. As citizens, people might well attempt to promote democratic goals—by, for example, calling for free air time for candidates in the late stages of campaigns—even if they do little to promote those goals in their purely individual capacities.

Indeed, the deliberative aspects of politics, bringing additional information and perspectives to bear, often affects people's judgments as these are expressed through governmental processes. A principal function of a democratic system is to ensure that through representative or participatory processes, new or submerged voices, or novel depictions of where interests lie and what they in fact are, are heard and understood. If representatives or citizens are able to participate in a collective discussion of broadcasting or the appropriate uses of the Internet, they can generate a far fuller and richer picture of the central social goals, and of how they might be served, than can be provided through individual decisions as registered in the market. It should hardly be surprising if preferences, values, and perceptions of what matters, to individuals and to societies, are changed as a result of that process.

Of course it cannot be denied that government officials have their own interests and biases, and that participants in politics might invoke public goals in order to serve their own private agendas. In the area of communications, not excluding the Internet, parochial pressures have often helped to dic-

129

tate public policy. In the end, it is indispensable to preserve free markets against those pressures. But if citizens are attempting to promote their own aspirations, they might well be able to make those markets work better; and it is certainly important to listen to what they have to say.

Unanimity and Majority Rule

Arguments based on citizens' collective desires are irresistible if the measure at issue is adopted unanimously—if all citizens are for it. But more serious difficulties are produced if (as is usual) the law imposes on a minority what it regards as a burden rather than a benefit. Suppose, for example, that a majority wants to require free television time for candidates or to have three hours of educational programming for children each week—but that a minority objects, contending that it is indifferent to speech by candidates, and that it does not care if there is more educational programming for children. It might be thought that those who perceive a need to bind themselves to some obligation, or to a course of action of some kind, should not be permitted to do so if the consequence is to bind others who perceive no such need.

Any interference with the preferences of the minority is indeed unfortunate, and in the end it might be a decisive objection. But we need to investigate the context. In general, it is difficult to see what argument there might be for an across-the-board rule against modest democratic efforts to improve the communications market. If the majority is prohibited from promoting its aspirations or vindicating its considered judgments through legislation, people will be less able to engage in democratic self-government. The choice is between the considered judgments of the majority and the preferences of the minority. I am not suggesting, of course, that the minority should be foreclosed where its rights are genuinely at risk.

Unhappy Sovereigns: The Consumption Treadmill

Throughout the discussion I have assumed that insofar as people are indeed acting as consumers, new communications technologies are an unambiguous boon. This is a widespread assumption, and it is easy to see why. If you want to buy anything at all, it has become much easier to do so. If you'd like a Toyota Camry, a Honda Accord, or a sports utility vehicle, many sites are available for the purpose; wallets, watches, and wristbands are easily found online; shirts and sweaters can be purchased in seconds. Nor is convenience the only point. As a result of the Internet, ordinary people have a much greater range of choices, and competitive pressures are, in a sense, far more intense for producers. Just to take one example, priceline.com allows you to "Name Your Own Price" for airline tickets, hotel rooms, groceries, new cars, mortgages, rental cars, sporting goods, strollers, swings, televisions, exercise equipment, and much more. Recall Anderson's celebration of "the long tail"; people with unusual tastes are now able to find what they want, overcoming the barriers of space that limit the options in bookstores, movie theaters, and much more.

Indeed the growth of options for consumers has been a prime engine behind the growth of the Internet. Consider a little history. In the early years, the list of the most popular sites was dominated by .edu domains. As late as 1996, no .com sites ranked among the top 15! By 1999—only three years later—the picture had fundamentally changed, to the point that the top-ranked .edu site (the University of Michigan)

131

ranked number 92. Only three of the fifteen top-ranked sites from January 1996 remained in the top rank three years later (AOL, Netscape, and Yahoo). And by that time, commercial enterprises had a substantial presence on the list. They have been growing most rapidly as well, to the point where there were nearly 25 million .com cites in January 2000, as compared to 6 million .edu sites, and under 1 million .gov sites. The increase, in sheer numbers and in proportions, has been remarkable since that time. In 2006, there were no fewer than 14,590,000,000 .com sites, accounting for about 40 percent of the total— compared to 2,490,000,000 .edu sites (less than 5 percent of the total), and 1,750,000,000 .gov sites (less than 4 percent of the total).

Insofar as the number of .coms is growing, it might seem clear that consumers, as consumers, are far better off as a result. On balance, they certainly are. But there is a qualification: extensive evidence shows that *our experience of many goods and services is largely a product of what other people have, and when there is a general improvement in everyone's consumer goods, people's well-being is increased little or not at all.*[7] Notwithstanding the evidence on its behalf, this might seem to be a positively weird suggestion. Isn't it obvious that better consumer goods are good for consumers? Actually it isn't so obvious. The reason is that people evaluate many goods by seeing how they compare to goods generally. If consumer goods as a whole are (say) 20 percent better, people are not going to be 20 percent happier, and they may not be happier at all.

To see the point, imagine that your current computer is the average computer from ten years ago. Chances are good that ten years ago, that computer was entirely fine, for you as for most other people. Chances are also good that if there had been no advances in computers, and if each of us had the same computer, in terms of quality, as we had ten years ago, little would be amiss. But in light of the massive improvement in computers in the last decade, you would undoubtedly be disappointed by continuing to own a computer from ten years before. Partly this is because it would seem hopelessly slow and infuriatingly inefficient, since the frame of reference has been set by much more advanced computers; those computers set the standard by which you evaluate what you own. Partly this is because your decade-old computer would not be able to interact well with modern ones, and it would place you at a serious disadvantage in dealing with others, not least in the marketplace.

This point need not depend on a claim that people are envious of their neighbors (though sometimes they are), or that people care a great deal about their status and how they are doing in comparison with others (though status is indeed important). For many goods, the most important point, developed by the economist Robert Frank, is that the frame of reference is set socially, not individually.[8] Our experience of what we have is determined by that frame of reference. What the Internet is doing is to alter the frame of reference, and by a large degree. This is not an unmixed blessing for consumers, even if it is a terrific development for many sellers.

To evaluate the Internet's effects on consumers, it is necessary only to see a simple point: when millions of consumers simultaneously find themselves with improved opportunities to find goods, they are certainly better off, but they are also likely to find themselves on a kind of "treadmill" in which each is continually trying to purchase more and better, simply in order to keep up with others and with the ever-shifting frame of reference. Indeed, what is true for computers is all the more true for countless other goods, including most of the vast array of products available on the Internet, such as sports utility vehicles, CD players, and televisions. Computers are evaluated socially, to be sure, but at least it can be said that fast and efficient ones might genuinely improve our lives, not least by enabling us to improve the operation of our democracy. But for many consumer goods, where the frame of reference is also provided socially, what really matters is how they compare to what other people have, and not how good they are in absolute terms. What would be a wonderful car or television in one time and place will seem ridiculously primitive in another.

In sum, the problem with the consumption treadmill, which is moving ever faster as a result of the Internet, is that despite growing expenditures and improved goods, the shift in the frame of reference means that consumers are unlikely to be much happier or better off. If the Internet is making it far easier for consumers to get better goods, or the same goods at a better price, they are certainly better off, perhaps even significantly so. But there is every reason to doubt that this is producing as much of an improvement in life, even for consumers, as we like to think.

This argument should not be misunderstood. Some "goods" actually do improve people's well-being, independently of shifts in the frame of reference. These goods tend to involve "inconspicuous consumption," from which people receive benefits apart from what other people have or do.[9] When people have more leisure time, or when they have a chance to exercise and keep in shape, or when they are able to spend more time with family and friends, their lives are likely to be better, whatever other people are doing. But when what matters is the frame set for social comparison, a society focused on better consumer goods will face a serious problem: people will channel far too many resources into the consumption "treadmill" and far too little into goods that are not subject to the treadmill effect, or that would otherwise be far better for society (such as improved protection against crime, environmental pollution, or assistance for poor people).

There is a growing body of research on "happiness," or subjective welfare, and it helps to support this point.[10] Perhaps the most striking finding is that substantial increases in Gross Domestic Product do not create noticeable increases in people's self-reported happiness. Even when economic growth is substantial, happiness in most countries is about the same as it was before. What matters far more is relative position: when people have less income and wealth than their neighbors, they tend to be less happy. Apparently money is a "positional good," in the sense that our experience of it depends on our position in the social hierarchy. (Health, by contrast, is not positional, or at least it is much less positional; if you're very sick, you feel very sick even if other people also feel very sick.) To be sure, people in very poor countries do show increases in self-reported happiness with real GDP growth. Moreover, those at the very bottom are happier when their absolute income increases, even if they stay at the bottom. But for most people in most nations, relative position greatly matters and absolute income does not.

It follows that the purchase of consumer goods and the opportunity to buy more and better do much less for people than they think. The emerging work on these topics raises many questions, and I do not attempt to answer them here. But insofar as consumers have an increasing range of options and can buy exactly what they want, it is far from clear that their lives are much better.

For present purposes my conclusions are simple. The Internet unquestionably makes purchases easier and more convenient for consumers. To this extent, it is a genuine boon for most of us. But it is less of a boon than we usually

135

think, particularly to the extent that it accelerates the consumption treadmill without making life much better for consumers of most goods. If citizens are reflective about their practices and their lives, they are entirely aware of this fact. As citizens, we might well choose to slow down the treadmill, or to ensure that resources that now keep it moving will be devoted to better uses. And insofar as citizens are attempting to accomplish that worthy goal, the idea of liberty should hardly stand in the way.

Democracy and Preferences

When people's preferences are a product of excessively limited options, there is a problem from the standpoint of freedom, and we do freedom a grave disservice by insisting on respect for preferences. When options are plentiful, things are much better. But there is also a problem, from the standpoint of freedom, when people's past choices lead to the development of preferences that limit their own horizons and their capacity for citizenship.

Consumers are not citizens, and it is a large error to conflate the two. One reason for the disparity is that the process of democratic choice often elicits people's aspirations. When we are thinking about what we as a nation should do—rather than what each of us as consumers should buy—we are often led to think of our larger, long-term goals. We may therefore hope to promote a high-quality communications market even if, as consumers, we seek "infotainment." Within the democratic process, we are also able to act as a group and not limited to our options as individuals. Acting as a group, we are thus in a position to solve various obstacles to dealing properly with issues that we cannot, without great difficulty, solve on our own.

These points obviously bear on a number of questions outside of the area of communications, such as environmental protection and antidiscrimination law. In many contexts, people, acting in their capacity as citizens, favor measures that diverge from the choices they make in their capacity as consumers. Of course it is important to impose constraints, usually in the form of rights, on what political majorities may do under this rationale. But if I am correct, one thing is clear: a system of limitless individual choices with respect to communications is not necessarily in the interest of citizenship and self-government, and efforts to reduce the resulting problems ought not to be rejected in freedom's name.

6

Blogs

ONE OF THE MORE striking developments of the early twenty-first century has been the rise of weblogs, which can serve to elicit and aggregate the information held by countless contributors. Weblogs, or "blogs," have been growing at a truly astounding rate—so much so that any current account will rapidly grow out of date. As of the present writing, there are over 55 million blogs, and over 40,000 new ones are created each day, with a new one every 2.2 seconds. (Question: How many blogs are created in the time it takes to read a short book?) In recent years, the most highly rated political blogs—including Atrios, Instapundit, and the Daily Kos—have received over tens of thousands of visitors *each day*.

You can easily find blogs on countless subjects. Often, of course, the real topic is the life of the author, in an unintended reimagining of the idea of the Daily Me; one survey finds that "the typical blog is written by a teenage girl who uses it twice a month to update her friends and classmates on happenings in her life."[1] Political blogs are a small percentage of the total, but they are plentiful, and they seem to be having a real influence on people's beliefs and judgments. In my own field of law, there are numerous blogs, and some of them are often quite good. For example, the Volokh Conspiracy and Balkinization offer clear and illuminating analyses of legal questions, often with amazing speed.

For most of those who write and read them, blogs can be a lot of fun. And if countless people are maintaining their own blogs, they should be able to act as fact-checkers and as supplemental information sources, not only for one another but also for prominent members of the mass media. If hundreds of thousands of people are reading the most prominent blogs, then errors should be corrected quickly. No one doubts that the blogosphere enables interested readers to find an astounding range of opinions and facts.

If the blogosphere is working well, we might understand it in two different ways. First, we might believe that the blogosphere serves as a huge market, in a way that supports the claims of those who claim that free markets can help society to obtain the widely dispersed information that individuals have. Second, we might think that the blogosphere operates as a kind of gigantic town meeting, in a way that fits well with the claims of those who speak of the operation of the well-functioning public sphere. On this second view, the world of blogs is helping to improve the operation of deliberative democracy, because it involves a great deal of citizen involvement and because arguments are often supported by facts and reasons.

These two understandings of the blogosphere lie behind many of the contemporary celebrations. Are the celebrations warranted?

On Prices

A prolific and accomplished blogger, federal court of appeals Judge Richard A. Posner has emphasized the ability of blogs to reveal dispersed bits of information. In Judge Posner's words:

> Blogging is . . . a fresh and striking exemplification of Friedrich Hayek's thesis that knowledge is widely distributed among peo-

139

ple and that the challenge to society is to create mechanisms for pooling that knowledge. The powerful mechanism that was the focus of Hayek's work, as of economists generally, is the price system (the market). The newest mechanism is the "blogosphere." . . . The Internet enables the instantaneous pooling (and hence correction, refinement, and amplification) of the ideas and opinions, facts and images, reportage and scholarship, generated by bloggers.[2]

I believe that Posner's argument is wrong, and that an investigation of his mistake can tell us a lot about operation of the blogosphere.

To understand Posner's argument, and what is wrong with it, we have to spend a little time with Friedrich Hayek, Posner's evident inspiration. Hayek's most important contribution to social thought, which bears on many of my concerns here, is captured in his short 1945 paper "The Use of Knowledge in Society."[3] Hayek claims that the great advantage of prices is that they aggregate both the information and the tastes of numerous people, incorporating far more material than could possibly be assembled by any central planner or board. Hayek emphasizes the unshared nature of information—the "dispersed bits of incomplete and frequently contradictory knowledge which all the separate individuals possess."[4] That knowledge certainly includes facts about products, but it also includes preferences and tastes, and all of these must be taken into account by a well-functioning market. Hayek stresses above all the "very important but unorganized knowledge which cannot possibly be called scientific in the sense of general rules: the knowledge of the particular circumstances of time and place."[5]

For Hayek, the key economic question is how to elicit that unorganized and dispersed knowledge. That problem cannot possibly be solved by any particular person or board. Central planners are unable to have access to all of the knowledge held by people in general. Taken as a whole, the knowledge held by those people is far greater than that held by even the most well-chosen experts. Hayek's central point is that when knowledge of relevant facts is dispersed among many people, prices act as an astonishingly concise and accurate aggregating device. They incorporate that dispersed knowledge, and in a sense also publicize it because the price itself operates as a signal to all.

At the same time, the price system has a wonderfully automatic quality, particularly in its capacity to respond to change. If fresh information shows that a product—a television, a car, a watch—doesn't always work, people's demand for it will rapidly fall, and so too the price. And when a product suddenly becomes more scarce, its users must respond to that fact, and the price will jump. In Hayek's view, free markets work remarkably well not because any participant can see all its features, but because the relevant information is communicated to everyone through prices.

Hence Hayek claims that it "is more than a metaphor to describe the price system as a kind of machinery for registering changes, or a system of telecommunications which enables individual produces to watch merely the movement of a few pointers."[6] Hayek describes this process as a marvel, and adds that he has chosen that word on purpose so as "to shock the reader out of the complacency with which we often take the working of the mechanism for granted."[7]

Priceless Words

We can see in this light why Judge Posner is so drawn to Hayek in his effort to understand the operation of the blogosphere. Hayek's concern is the dispersed nature of information in society; he believes that the price system operates to elicit that information. No one can doubt that the blogosphere certainly allows a lot of knowledge, including local knowledge, to come to public light. In a general sense, that process might well be seen as a way of collecting information and offering it to those who might respond to it.

But the analogy immediately runs into big problems. Most important, the blogosphere does not produce prices, which aggregate in one place a wide range of opinions and tastes. The aggregating device of the market, Hayek's marvel, cannot be found there. What is offered instead is a stunningly diverse range of claims, perspectives, rants, insights, lies, facts, non-facts, sense, and nonsense. Spend just a little time on blogs involving politics or law, and the problem will become immediately clear. Even Hayek's admirers are willing to admit that some prices, especially those of stocks, are not so sensible; but as compared with discussion of public policy on the blogosphere, the world of prices and the stock market are marvels of rationality and order.

True enough, many blogs aggregate a lot of information; instapundit.com, for example, assembles material from many sources. We might even consider the most elite bloggers, who gather material from elsewhere in the blogosphere, as an aggregating mechanism of sorts. Daniel Drezner and Henry Farrell have shown that because of the networked structure of the blogosphere, "only a few blogs are likely to become focal points," but those few blogs "offer both a means of filtering interesting blog posts from less interesting ones, and a focal point at which bloggers with interesting posts and potential readers of these posts can coordinate."[8] But this mechanism does not vindicate Posner's analogy. Some of the elite or "focal point" bloggers have their own biases. Many of them are primarily interested in cherry-picking items of opinion or information that reinforce their preexisting views. In other words, we lack a blog that succeeds in correcting errors and assembling truths. Those who consult blogs will learn a great deal, but they will have a tough time separating falsehoods from facts.

There is another point. Participants in the blogospere often lack an economic incentive. If they spread falsehoods, or simply offer their opinion, they usually sacrifice little or nothing. Maybe their reputation will suffer, but maybe not; maybe the most dramatic falsehoods will draw attention and hence readers. True, some bloggers attract advertising, and they have a stake in preserving their credibility. But most bloggers do not, and it is hardly clear that the best way to attract advertising revenues is to tell the truth. Many advertisers on political blogs are themselves trying to sell products designed to appeal to those with strong partisan beliefs. They are unlikely to object to exaggerations and semifalsehoods that appeal to the prejudices of their target audiences.

By their very nature, blogs offer rival and contentious positions on facts as well as values. In many ways, this is a virtue. People who are curious can find a wide range of views, including those that oppose their own. But if truth is to emerge, it is because of the competition of the marketplace of ideas, and this particular marketplace is far from perfect. One of the undeniable effects of blogs is to spread misunderstandings and mistakes. This point leads to another possible understanding of blogs, closely connected to my central concerns here—an understanding that is rooted in the idea of deliberative democracy.

143

Blogs (Not) as Deliberative Democracy

To some extent, the blogosphere is a place for deliberation, and perhaps a deliberative conception will do much better than one rooted in markets and prices. Consider Aristotle's suggestion that when diverse groups "all come together . . . they may surpass—collectively and as a body, although not individually—the quality of the few best. . . . When there are many who contribute to the process of deliberation, each can bring his share of goodness and moral prudence; . . . some appreciate one part, some another, and all together appreciate all."[9] Here, then, is a clear suggestion that many minds, deliberating together, may improve on "the quality of the few best." More recently, John Rawls writes of the same possibility: "The benefits from discussion lie in the fact that even representative legislators are limited in knowledge and the ability to reason. No one of them knows everything the others know, or can make all the same inferences that they can draw in concert. Discussion is a way of combining information and enlarging the range of arguments."[10]

Jürgen Habermas, elaborating these themes, stresses norms and practices designed to allow victory by "the better argument":

> Rational discourse is supposed to be public and inclusive, to grant equal communication rights for participants, to require sincerity and to diffuse any kind of force other than the forceless force of the better argument. This communicative structure is expected to create a deliberative space for the mobilization of the best available contributions for the most relevant topics.[11]

Habermas has explored the idea of an "ideal speech situation," in which all participants attempt to seek the truth; do

144

not behave strategically; and accept a norm of equality.[12] Certainly it can be said that as compared to many alternatives, the blogosphere is both "public and inclusive," and grants communication rights to countless participants. Perhaps the blogosphere can be said to operate, at least to some degree, in this idealized fashion, in a way that will promote the emergence of "the better argument."

In view of what we know about group polarization, however, it should be clear that this happy view of the blogosphere faces a big problem. Drezner and Farrell emphasize its networked structure, in which ideas from less popular blogs can "bubble up" to much larger audiences. But a serious question is whether people are mostly reading blogs that conform to their own preexisting beliefs. If so, the truth is not likely to emerge, and polarization is nearly inevitable. Liberals, reading liberal blogs, will end up being more liberal; conservatives will become more conservative if they restrict themselves to conservative blogs. Recall the Colorado experiment discussed in chapter 3, in which liberals spoke with liberals and conservatives with conservatives—and in which both groups ended up more extreme than they were when they started to talk.

It is entirely reasonable to think that something of this kind finds itself replicated in the blogosphere every day. Indeed some bloggers, and many readers of blogs, try to create echo chambers. Because of self-sorting, people are often reading like-minded points of view, in a way that can breed greater confidence, more uniformity within groups, and more extremism. Note in this regard that shared identities are often salient on the blogosphere, in a way that makes polarization both more likely and more likely to be large. On any day of any year, it is easy to find unjustified rage, baseless attacks on people's motivations, and ludicrous false statements of fact in the blogosphere. From the democratic point of the view, this is nothing to celebrate.

Of course the quality of bloggers is immensely variable, and some of them are very good, in part because they take account of reasonable counterarguments. (I have mentioned the Volokh Conspiracy and Balkinization; outside of law, Tyler Cowen's Marginal Revolution stands out.) Posner may misuse Hayek, but he is right to suggest that blogging can operate as an extraodinary method for collecting dispersed knowledge. Sheer numbers play a beneficial role here. Information aggregation is likely to work best when many minds are involved, but it is also important that reasons and information are being exchanged in a way that can lead to corrections and real creativity. To some extent, this is happening already. I have not denied that we are better off with blogs than without them. But it is a big stretch to celebrate blogs as an incarnation of deliberative ideals.

Evidence

Some of the claims I have been offering here are theoretical and conceptual, but they also have an empirical dimension. Perhaps empirical work could show that the blogosphere often does elicit and aggregate information, perhaps by correcting rather than disseminating widespread social errors. Certainly empirical evidence could demonstrate that the risk of group polarization is small—if, for example, people actually read a wide range of views, and not simply those with whom they antecedently agree.

What do we actually know about the blogosphere? All too little. The empirical analysis remains in its earliest stages. Of course there are many anecdotes. Drawing from the account of blogging enthusiast Hugh Hewitt,[13] let us consider a few:

- Bloggers deserve significant credit for the 2004 "Rathergate" scandal, in which Dan Rather used what seemed to be authentic memoranda to offer embarrassing disclosures about the military service of President George W. Bush. Careful bloggers showed that the memoranda could not possibly be authentic. Only one day after the broadcast, a blogger known as Buckhead wrote, "Every single one of these memos to file is in a proportionally spaced font, probably Palatino or Times New Roman. In 1972 people used typewriters for this sort of thing, and typewriters used monospaced fonts. . . . I am saying these documents are forgeries, run through a copier for 15 generations to make them look old." Additional bloggers worked hard to confirm the accusation. As Hewitt notes, bloggers "exposed the fraud with breathtaking speed and finality."[14]
- In 2002, Trent Lott, Senate majority leader, spoke at a birthday party for Senator Strom Thurmond. Lott said of Mississippi, his own state, "When Strom Thurmond ran for president, we voted for him. We're proud of it. And if the rest of the country had followed our lead, we wouldn't have had all these problems over all these years, either." This was a genuinely scandalous statement; Thurmond had run on a racist, pro-segregation platform, and the Senate majority leader seemed to be saying that if Thurmond had won, the nation would have been problem-free. But somehow the remarks were ignored—except on the blogosphere. A blogger named Atrios gave serious coverage to the comments, which were then picked up on talkingpointsmemo.com,

and the building momentum proved unstoppable. Lott was forced to resign as majority leader.

• In 1979, John Kerry said, "I remember spending Christmas Eve of 1968 five miles across the Cambodian border being shot at by our South Vietnamese allies who were drunk and celebrating Christmas." During the 2004 election, the blogosphere was full of stories about whether Kerry had really spent Christmas Eve in Cambodia, and indeed whether he had been in Cambodia at all. Focussing on the claim of Christmas Eve in Cambodia, one blogger, RogerLSimon.com, objected to the prospect of having someone "who sounds like a pathetic barroom blowhard" as president of the United States, especially "in a time of war. People like this start to believe their own lies." A liberal blogger, Matthew Yglesias, said, "It certainly looks bad from here, and I haven't seen a good explanation yet, perhaps because there isn't one." Eventually the Kerry campaign acknowledged that Kerry had not been in Cambodia on Christmas in 1968. As Hewitt writes, "The Christmas-Eve-not-in-Cambodia became shorthand for Kerry's fantasy life, and suddenly the Swift Vets," who had savagely attacked Kerry's honesty and patriotism, "had credibility, as Internet donations flowed into their coffers."[15]

Whatever one thinks of each of these events, bloggers appear to have influenced the public stage, driving media coverage and affecting national perceptions of national questions. Unfortunately, there is also good evidence that many bloggers are mostly linking to like-minded others—and that when they link to opinions that diverge from their own, it is often to cast ridicule and scorn on them.

One study explores the degree to which conservative and liberal bloggers are interacting with each other. Focusing on 1,400 blogs, the study finds that 91 percent of the links are to like-minded sites.[16] Hence the two sides sort themselves into identifiable communities. For example, powerlineblog.com, a conservative blog, has links from only twenty-five liberal blogs—but from 195 conservative blogs. Dailykos.com, a liberal blog, has links from 46 conservative blogs—but from 292 liberal blogs. In the aggregate, the behavior of conservative bloggers is more noteworthy in this regard; they link to one another far more often and in a denser pattern. The study's authors also examined about 40 "A-List" blogs, and here too they found a great deal of segregation. Sources were cited almost exclusively by one side or the other. Those sites with identifiable political commitments, such as Salon.com and NationalReview.com, were almost always cited by blogs on the same side of the political spectrum.

Another study, by Eszter Hargittai, Jason Gallo, and Matt Kane, offers more detailed support for the same general conclusions.[17] Examining the behavior of forty popular blogs—half liberal and half conservative—Hargittai and her coauthors find that like-minded views receive a great deal of reinforcement. On the "blogrolls," referring readers to other blogs, conservatives are far more likely to list other conservatives, and liberals are far more likely to list other liberals. When blogs refer to discussions by other bloggers, they usually cite like-minded others. To be sure, there is a significant amount of cross-citation as well. But—and here is perhaps the most striking finding—a plurality of cross-citations simply cast contempt on the views that are being cited! Only a quarter of cross-ideological posts involve genuine substantive discussion. In this way, real deliberation is often occurring within established points of view, but only infrequently across them.

149

Polarized Blogs

The general conclusion is that in the blogosphere, there is a significant divide between politically identifiable communities. Liberals link mostly to liberals and conservatives link mostly to conservatives. Much of the time, they do not even discuss the same topics. Of course, it is true that many people are using the blogosphere not to strengthen their antecedent convictions, and not to waste their time, but to learn about different views and new topics. The blogosphere increases the range of available information and perspectives, and this is a great virtue, above all for curious and open-minded people. There are networks here with multiple connections, not entirely segregated communities. But if linking behavior on blogs can be taken as a proxy for how people are using the blogosphere, it is reasonable to think that many readers are obtaining one-sided views of political issues. For many people, blunders, confusion, and extremism are highly likely, not in spite of the blogosphere but because of it.

7

What's Regulation? A Plea

On May 4, 2000, my computer received an odd email, entitled LOVE LETTER FOR YOU. The email contained an attachment. When I opened the email, I learned that the attachment was a love letter. The sender of the email was someone I'd never met—as it happens, an employee at Princeton University Press, the publisher of this very book. I thought I probably should look at this love letter, so I clicked once. But it occurred to me that this might not be a love letter at all, and so I didn't click twice.

I had been sent the ILOVEYOU virus, which infected the world's computers in May 2000. This was a particularly fiendish virus. If you opened it, you received not only a love note but also a special surprise: your computer would send the same love note to every address in your computer's address book. For many people, this was funny, in a way, but also extremely awful and embarrassing—not least for a law professor, finding himself in the position, much worse than uncomfortable, of sending countless unwelcome love letters to both students and colleagues.

The ILOVEYOU virus was capable of many impressive feats. For example, it could delete files. It was apparently capable of mutating, so that many people found themselves, not with love letters, but with notes about Mother's Day—less intriguing and more innocuous, perhaps, than a love letter, but

151

also capable of mischief, as when an employee at a random company finds himself sending dozens of Mother's Day notes to friends and colleagues, many of them near-strangers (and not mothers). The ILOVEYOU virus was apparently capable of mutating into, or in any case was shortly followed by, its own apparent cure, with matching attachment: HOW TO PROTECT YOURSELF FROM THE ILOVEYOU BUG! This attachment turned out to be a virus too.

The worldwide costs of the ILOVEYOU went well beyond embarrassment. In Belgium, ATMs were disabled. Throughout Europe, email servers were shut down. Significant costs were imposed on the taxpayers as well—partly because affected computers included those of government, partly because governments all over the world cooperated in enforcement efforts. In London, Parliament was forced to close down its servers, and email systems were crippled in the United States Congress. At the U.S. Department of Defense, four classified email systems were corrupted. The ultimate price tag has been estimated at over $10 billion. Ultimately the Federal Bureau of Investigation traced the origin of this virus to a young man in the Philippines.

A Common View

My discussion thus far has involved the social foundations of a well-functioning system of free expression—what such a system requires if it is to work well. But it would be possible for a critic to respond that government and law have no legitimate role in responding to any problems that might emerge from individual choices. On this view, a free society respects those choices and avoids "regulation," even if what results from free choices is quite undesirable; that is what freedom is all about.

152

If the claim here is really about freedom, I have already attempted to show what is wrong with it. Freedom should not
always be identified with "choices." Of course free societies
usually respect free choices. But sometimes choices reflect,
and can in fact produce, a lack of freedom. But perhaps the
argument is rooted in something else: a general hostility to any
form of government regulation. This is, of course, a pervasive
and perhaps growing kind of hostility. A quite common argument is that legal interference with the communications market should be rejected, simply because it is a form of government regulation, and to be disfavored for exactly that reason.

Many people make such an argument about the emerging
television market. With the extraordinary growth in the number of channels, they argue, scarcity is no longer a reason for
regulation; shouldn't government simply leave the scene?
Shouldn't it eliminate regulation altogether? The same argument is being made about the Internet, indeed more force-
fully, with the suggestion that it should be taken as a kind of
government-free zone. Thus cyberspace activist John Perry
Barlow produced, in 1996, an influential Declaration of the
Independence of Cyberspace, urging, among other things,
"Governments of the Industrial World . . . I ask you of the
past to leave us alone. You are not welcome among us. You
have no sovereignty where we gather. . . .You have no moral
right to rule us nor do you possess any methods of enforcement we have true reason to fear."[1]

An Incoherent View: Regulation and Law Everywhere

The story of the ILOVEYOU virus suggests that this argument
is quite ridiculous. Could any sensible person support a system in which government was banned from helping to protect

153

against computer viruses? But the story of the ILOVEYOU virus also suggests something more interesting and more subtle. The real problem is that opposition to government regulation is incoherent.

There is no avoiding "regulation" of the communications market—of television, print media, and the Internet. The question is not whether we will have regulation; it is what kind of regulation we will have. Newspapers and magazines, radio and television stations, and websites—all of these benefit from government regulation every day. Indeed, a system of regulation-free speech is barely imaginable. Those who complain most bitterly about proposed regulation are often those who most profit, often financially, from current regulation. They depend not only on themselves but also on government and law. What they are complaining about is not regulation as such—they need regulation—but a regulatory regime from which they would benefit less than they do under the current one.

To see the point, begin by considering the actual status of broadcast licensees, in both television and radio, for the last six decades and more. Broadcasters do not have their licenses by nature or divine right. Their licenses are emphatically a product of government grants—legally conferred property rights, in the form of monopolies over frequencies, originally given out for free to ABC, CBS, NBC, and PBS. In the early 1990s, government went so far as to give existing owners a right to produce digital television—what was called, by Senator Robert Dole and many others, a "$70 billion giveaway." This gift from the public—the grant of property rights via government, in this case for free rather than through auction—is simply a highly publicized way in which government and law are responsible for the rights of those who own and operate radio and television stations.

154

Though we often don't think of them this way, property rights, when conferred by law, are a quintessential form of government regulation. They create power and they limit power. They determine who owns what, and they say who may do what to whom. In the case of radio and television broadcasters, they impose firm limits on others, who may not, under federal law, speak on CBS or NBC unless CBS or NBC allows them to do so. It makes no sense to decry government regulation of television broadcasters when it is government regulation that is responsible for the very system at issue. That system could not exist without a complex regulatory framework from which broadcasters benefit.

Nor is it merely the fact that government created the relevant property rights in the first instance. Government also protects these rights, at taxpayers' expense, via civil and criminal law, both of which prohibit people from gaining access to what broadcasters "own." If you try to get access to the public via CBS, to appear on its channels without its permission, you will have committed a crime, and the FBI itself is likely to become involved. There is considerable irony in the fact that for many years, broadcasters have complained about government regulation; government regulation is responsible for their rights in the first place. There is a particular irony in broadcasters' vociferous objections to the quite modest public-interest requirements that have been imposed on them, in the form of (for example) requirements for educational programming for children, attention to public issues, and an opportunity for diverse views to speak.

Of course broadcasters may have some legitimate objections here, at least if they can show that meeting these requirements does little good. But what is not legitimate is for broadcasters to act as if public-interest regulation imposes law and government where neither existed before. Broadcast-

155

ers could not exist, in their current form, if not for the fact that law and government are emphatically present. It is law and government that make it possible for them to make money in the first place.[2]

What is true for broadcasters is also true for newspapers and magazines, though here the point is less obvious. Newspapers and magazines also benefit from government regulation through the grant of property rights, again protected at taxpayers' expense. Suppose, for example, that you would like to publish something in the *Washington Post* or in *Time* magazine. Perhaps you believe that one or the other has neglected an important perspective and you would like to fill the gap. If you request publication and are refused, you are entirely out of luck. The most important reason is that the law has created a firm right of exclusion—a legal power to exclude others—and given this right to both newspapers and magazines. The law is fully prepared to back up that right of exclusion with both civil and criminal safeguards. No less than CBS and ABC, the *Washington Post* and *Time* magazine are beneficiaries of legal regulation, preventing people from saying what they want to say where they want to say it.

Now it may be possible to imagine a world of newspapers and magazines without legal protection of this kind. This would be a world without regulation. But what kind of world would this be? Without the assistance of the law, all sides would be left with a struggle to show superior force. In such a world, people would be able to publish where they wanted if and only if they had the power to insist. Newspapers and magazines would be able to exclude would-be authors so long as they had enough power to do so. Who can know who would win that struggle? (Perhaps you have a gun, or a small private army, and can force the *Washington Post* to publish you at gunpoint.) In our society, access to newspapers and

156

magazines is determined not by power but by legal regulation, allocating and enforcing property rights, and doing all this at public expense.

The Case of the Internet: Some Historical Notes

Despite the widespread claim that the Internet is and should be free of government controls, things are not much different in cyberspace. Here too regulation and government support have been omnipresent. But there are some interesting wrinkles in this context, and they are worth rehearsing here, because they bear on the relationship between regulation and the Internet, and because they are noteworthy in their own right.

Consider history first. This supposedly government-free zone was a creation not of the private sector but of the national government. Indeed, the private sector was given several chances to move things along, but refused, in a way that shows a remarkable lack of foresight. We are used to hearing tales of the unintended bad consequences of government action. The Internet is an unintended good consequence of government action, by the Department of Defense no less. Beginning in the 1960s, the Advanced Research Project Agency (ARPA) of the Department of Defense created a new computer network, originally called the Arpanet, with the specific purpose of permitting computers to interact with one another, thus allowing defense researchers at various universities to share computing resources. In 1972, hundreds and then thousands of early users began to discover email as a new basis for communication. In the early 1970s, the government sought to sell off the Arpanet to the private sector, contacting AT&T to see if it wanted to take over the system. The

157

company declined, concluding that the Arpanet technology was incompatible with the AT&T network. (So much for the prescience of the private sector.)

Eventually the Arpanet—operating under the auspices of the federal government, in the form of the National Science Foundation—expanded to multiple uses. By the late 1980s, a number of new networks emerged, some far more advanced than the Arpanet, and the term "Internet" came to be used for the federally subsidized network consisting of many linked networks running the same protocols. In 1989 the Arpanet was transferred to regional networks throughout the country. A key innovation came one year later, when researchers at CERN, the European Laboratory for Particle Physics near Geneva, created the World Wide Web, a multimedia branch of the Internet. CERN researchers attempted to interest private companies in building the World Wide Web, but they declined ("too complicated"), and Tim Berners-Lee, the lead researcher and web inventor, had to build it on his own.

Hard as it now is to believe, the Internet began to become commercial only in 1992, as a result of the enactment of new legislation removing restrictions on commercial activity. It was around that time that direct government funding was largely withdrawn, but indirect funding and support continues. In 1995, the backbone of the national network was sold to a private consortium of corporations, and the government gave one company the exclusive right to register domain names (you can now buy names from a range of sellers). Originally created by the government, the Internet is now largely free of ongoing federal supervision—but with the important exceptions of guaranteed property rights and various restrictions on unlawful speech (such as conspiracy and child pornography).

Perhaps all this seems abstract. But the basic point lies at the very heart of the most fundamental of current debates about Internet policy. Consider, for example, an online exchange connected with an Internet symposium in the *American Prospect* in 2000. Eric S. Raymond, a highly influential developer and theorist of open-source software, sharply opposes "government regulation" and endorses "laissez faire" and "voluntary norms founded in enlightened self-interest." Stanford law professor and Internet specialist Lawrence Lessig, writing in very much the same terms as those urged here, responds that "contract law, rightly limited property rights, antitrust law, the breakup of AT&T" are also "regulations," made possible by "governmental policy." Answering Lessig, Raymond is mostly aghast. He acknowledges that he has no disagreement if the term regulation is meant to include "not active coercive intervention but policies which I and hackers in general agree with him are *not* coercive, such as the enforcement of property law and contract rights." But to Raymond, who purports to speak for a large "community consensus," the use of the term "regulation" to include this kind of law reflects a deep confusion in Lessig's "model of the world." "Contract and property law contain no proper names; they formalize an equilibrium of power between equals before the law and are good things; regulation privileges one party designated by law to dictate outcomes by force and is at best a very questionable thing. The one is no more like the other than a handshake is like a fist in the face."

Raymond is stating a widespread view; but the deep confusion is his, not Lessig's. Property law and contract rights are unquestionably "coercive" and entirely "active." These rights do not appear in nature, at least not in terms that are acceptable for human society. When would-be speakers are subject to a jail sentence for invading property rights, coercion is un-

159

questionably involved. This is not true only for homeless people, whose very status as such is unquestionably a product of law. Even those who create open-source software rely heavily on property law—in fact, contract law (through licenses) and at least some form of copyright law to control what happens to their software. Anyone who is punished for violating the copyright law, or for intruding on the "space" of CBS or a website owner, is coerced within any reasonable understanding of the term.

Nor do contract and property law merely "formalize an equilibrium of power." By conferring rights, they *create* an equilibrium of power—an equilibrium that would not and could not exist without "active" choices by government. In a genuine anarchy, in which everything was left to force, who knows what the equilibrium would look like, with respect to software, on the Internet or anywhere else? Contract law and property law are good, even wonderful things. But to many people much of the time, they are no mere handshake, but much more like "a fist in the face."

The Case of the Internet: Regulation Again

Simply because government creates and enforces property rights in cyberspace, the Internet, no less than ordinary physical spaces, remains pervaded by government regulation. Of course this does not mean that government should be permitted to do whatever it wants. But it does mean that the real question is what kind of regulation to have, not whether to have regulation.

As a result of the Love Bug and other viruses, considerable attention has been given in recent years to the risk and the reality of "cyberterrorism"—not only through email attachments, but also when "hackers" invade websites in order to disable them, or to post messages of their own choosing. According to one estimate, computer viruses cost the United States $13 billion each year.[3] But serious disruptions do not occur often. Why not? A key reason is that they are against the law. A complex framework of state, federal, and international law regulates behavior on the Internet, above all by giving site owners an entitlement to be free from trespass. These entitlements are created publicly and enforced at public expense. Indeed, immense resources—billions of dollars, including massive efforts by the Federal Bureau of Investigation—are devoted to the protection of these property rights. And when cyberterrorism does occur, everyone knows that the government is going to intervene to protect property rights, in part by ferreting out the relevant lawbreakers, in part by prosecuting them.

If we want, we might decline to call this government "regulation." But this would be a matter of semantics. When government creates and protects rights, and when it forbids people from doing what they want to do, it is regulating within any standard meaning of the term. The Internet is hardly an anarchy, or regulation-free. The reason is that governments stand ready to protect those whose property rights are at stake.

In this way the system of rights on the Internet is no different, in principle, from the system of rights elsewhere. But the Internet does present one complication. In ordinary space, it is not really possible, as a practical matter, to conceive of a system of property rights without a large government presence. Such a system would mean that property holders would have to resort to self-help, as through the hiring of private police forces; and for most property owners, including broadcasters, newspapers, and magazines, this is not really feasible. But something like it is at least a pragmatic possibility on the Internet. We might think, for example, that government could simply step out of the picture and enable site owners to qualify as such only to the extent that they can use their technological capacities to exclude others. In such a system, the website of Amazon.com would be run and operated by Amazon.com, but it would be free from outsiders only to the extent that the owners of Amazon.com could use technology to maintain their property rights. Amazon.com, in sum, would have a kind of sovereignty as a result of technology rather than law, and perhaps it could ensure this sovereignty through technology alone.

Because of current technological capacities, this is not an unimaginable state of affairs. Perhaps many people can protect themselves well enough from invaders, cyberterrorists, and others without needing the help of government. But even on the Internet, it would not make much sense to force people to rely on technology alone, in light of the great value of civil and criminal law as an aid to the enjoyment of property rights. In any case this imaginary world of self-help is not the world in which we live. The owners of websites, no less than the owners of everything else, benefit by government regulation; and without it, they would not really be owners at all.

Regulation Everywhere, Thank Goodness

None of these points should be taken as an argument against those forms of regulation that establish and guarantee property rights. On the contrary, a well-functioning system of free expression *needs* property rights. Such a system is likely to be much better if the law creates and protects owners of newspapers, magazines, broadcasting stations, and websites. Property rights make these institutions far more secure and stable and, for precisely this reason, produce much more in the way of speech.

In the Communist nations of the Soviet era, communications outlets were publicly owned, and all holdings were subject to governmental reallocation; it is an understatement to say that free speech could not flourish in such an environment. Thus the economist Friedrich Hayek, the greatest critic of socialism in the twentieth century, emphasized the omnipresence of legal regulation no less than I have here. As Hayek saw, an emphasis on the omnipresence of regulation is no challenge to a system rooted in property rights: "In no system that could be rationally defended would the state just do nothing," Hayek argued. "An effective competitive system needs an intelligently designed and continuously adjusted legal framework as much as any other."[4]

Nor does anything I have said suggest that it would be appropriate, or even legitimate, for government to control the content of what appears in newspapers and magazines, by saying, for example, that they must cover presidential elections, or offer dissenting opinions a right of reply. But any objection to such requirements must be based on something other than the suggestion that they would interfere with some law-free zone—that requirements of this sort would introduce a government presence where government had been absent before. Government has been there already, and it is still there, and we are much better off for that. If government is trying to do something new or different, one question is whether what it is trying to do would improve or impair democracy or the system of freedom of speech. That question cannot be resolved by reference to complaints about government regulation in the abstract.

163

If government is attempting to regulate television or radio in their contemporary forms, or some technology that combines or transcends them, it makes no sense to say that the attempt should fail because a free society opposes government regulation as such. No free society opposes that. Government regulation of speech, at least in the form of property rights that shut out would-be speakers, is a pervasive part of a system of freedom that respects, and therefore creates, rights of exclusion for owners of communications outlets.

Here, then, is my plea: when we are discussing possible approaches to the Internet or other new communications technologies, we should never suggest that one route involves government regulation and that another route does not. Statements of this kind produce confusion about what we are now doing and about our real options. And the confusion is far from innocuous. It puts those who are asking how to improve the operation of the speech market at a serious disadvantage. A democratic public should be permitted to discuss the underlying questions openly and pragmatically, and without reference to self-serving myths invoked by those who benefit, every hour of every day, from the exercise of government power on their behalf.

8

Freedom of Speech

Were those responsible for the ILOVEYOU virus protected by the free-speech principle? It would be silly to say that they are. But if this form of speech may be regulated, what are the limits on government's power?

Consider a case involving not email but a website—a case that may, in some ways, turn out to be emblematic of the future. The site in question had a dramatic name: "The Nuremberg Files." It began, "A coalition of concerned citizens throughout the USA is cooperating in collecting dossiers on abortionists in anticipation that one day we may be able to hold them on trial for crimes against humanity." The site contained a long list of "Alleged Abortionists and Their Accomplices," with the explicit goal of recording "the name of every person working in the baby slaughter business in the United States of America." The list included the names, home addresses, and license-plate numbers of many doctors who performed abortions, and also included the names of their spouses and children.

So far, perhaps, so good. But three of these doctors had been killed. Whenever a doctor was killed, the website showed a line drawn through his name. The site also included a set of "wanted posters," Old West—style, with photographs of doctors with the word "Wanted" under each one. A group of doctors brought suit, contending the practices of which this site was a part amounted in practice to "a hit list" with death threats and intimidation. The jury awarded them over $100 million in damages; the verdict was upheld on appeal, though the dollar award was reduced substantially (it remained in the millions of dollars).

Should the free-speech principle have protected the Nuremberg Files? Maybe it should have. But if you think so, would you allow a website to post names and addresses of doctors who performed abortions, with explicit instructions about how and where to kill them? Would you allow a website to post bomb-making instructions? To post such instructions alongside advice about how and where to use the bombs? To show terrorists exactly where and how to strike? As we have seen, there is nothing fanciful about these questions. Dozens of sites now contain instructions about how to make bombs— though to my knowledge, none of them tells people how and where to use them. If you have no problem with bomb-making instructions on websites, you might consider some other questions. Does your understanding of free speech allow people to work together at a site called pricefixing.com, through which competitors can agree to set prices and engage in other anticompetitive practices? (I made that one up.) Does your understanding of free speech allow people to make unauthorized copies of movies, music, and books, and to give or sell those copies to dozens, thousands, or millions of others? (I didn't make that one up.)

My basic argument here is that the free-speech principle, properly understood, is not an absolute and that it allows government to undertake a wide range of restrictions on what people want to say on the Internet. However the hardest questions should be resolved, the government can regulate computer viruses, criminal conspiracy, and explicit incitement to engage in criminal acts, at least if the incitement is likely to be effective. In my view, it would also be acceptable for government to require broadcasters to provide educational programming for children on television, as in fact it now does; to mandate free air time for candidates for public office; and to regulate contributions to and expenditures on political campaigns, at least within certain boundaries.

This is not the place for a full discussion of constitutional doctrines relating to freedom of expression. But in the process of showing the democratic roots of the system of free expression, I attempt to provide an outline of the basic constitutional principles.[1]

Emerging Wisdom? Televisions as Toasters

An emerging view is that the First Amendment to the Constitution requires government to respect consumer sovereignty. Indeed, the First Amendment is often treated as if it incorporates the economic ideal—as if it is based on the view that consumer choice is what the system of communications is all about. Although it is foreign to the original conception of the free-speech principle, this view can be found in many places in current law.

For one thing, it helps to explain the constitutional protection given to commercial advertising. This protection is exceedingly recent. Until 1976,[2] the consensus within the Supreme Court and the legal culture in general was that the First Amendment did not protect commercial speech at all. Since that time, commercial speech has come to be treated more and more like ordinary speech, to the point where Justice Thomas has even doubted whether the law should distinguish at all between commercial and political speech.[3] To date, Justice Thomas has not prevailed on this count. But the Court's commercial-speech decisions often strike down restrictions on advertising, and for that reason, those decisions are best seen as a way of connecting the idea of consumer sovereignty with the First Amendment itself.

Belonging in the same category is the frequent constitutional hostility to campaign-finance regulation. The Supreme Court has held that financial expenditures on behalf of political candidates are generally protected by the free-speech principle—and in what seems to me an act of considerable hubris, the Court has also held that it is illegitimate for government to try to promote political equality by imposing ceilings on permissible expenditures.[4] The inequality that comes from divergences in wealth is not, on the Court's view, a proper subject for democratic control. According to the Court, campaign-finance restrictions cannot be justified by reference to equality at all. It is for this reason that candidate *expenditures* from candidates' personal funds may not be regulated. It is also for this reason that restrictions on campaign *contributions* from one person to a candidate can be regulated only as a way of preventing the reality or appearance of corruption.

The constitutional debate over campaign-finance regulation remains complex and unresolved, and the members of the Supreme Court are badly divided.[5] Some of the justices would further reduce the government's existing authority to regulate campaign contributions, on the theory that such contributions lie at the heart of what the free-speech principle protects. Here too an idea of consumer sovereignty seems to be at work. In many of the debates over campaign expenditures and contributions, the political process itself is being treated as a kind of market in which citizens are seen as consumers, expressing their will not only through votes and statements but also through money. I do not mean to suggest

that the government should be able to impose whatever restrictions it wishes. I mean only to notice, and to question,
the idea that the political domain should be seen as a market
and the influential claim that government is entirely disabled
from responding to the translation of economic inequality
into political equality.

Even more relevant for present purposes is the widespread
suggestion, with some support in current constitutional law,
that the free-speech principle forbids government from in-
terfering with the communications market by, for example,
attempting to draw people's attention to serious issues or regulating the content of what appears on television networks.[6]
To be sure, everyone agrees that the government is permitted
to create and protect property rights, even if this means that
speech will be regulated as a result. We have seen that the
government may give property rights to websites and broadcasters; there is no constitutional problem with that. Everyone also agrees that the government is permitted to control
monopolistic behavior and thus to enforce antitrust law,
which is designed to ensure genuinely free markets in communications. Structural regulation, not involving direct control of speech but intended to make sure that the market
works well, is usually unobjectionable. Hence government
can create copyright law and, at least within limits, forbid unauthorized copying. (There is, however, an extremely important and active debate about how to reconcile copyright
law and the free-speech principle.)[7] But if government attempts to require television broadcasters to cover public issues, or to provide free air time for candidates, or to ensure a
certain level of high-quality programming for children, many
people will claim that the First Amendment is being violated.

What lies beneath the surface of these debates?

Two Free-Speech Principles

We might distinguish here between the free-speech principle as it operates in courts and the free-speech principle as it operates in public debate. As far as courts are concerned, there is as yet no clear answer to many of the constitutional questions that would be raised by government efforts to make the speech market work better. For example, we do not really know, as a matter of constitutional law, whether government can require educational and public-affairs programming on television. The Court allowed such regulation when three or four television stations dominated the scene, but it has left open the question of whether such regulation would be legitimate today.[8] As a matter of prediction, the most that can be said is that there is a reasonable chance that the Court would permit government to adopt modest initiatives, so long as it was promoting goals associated with deliberative democracy.

Indeed the Court has been very cautious, and selfconsciously so, about laying down firm rules governing the role of the free-speech principle on new technologies. The Court is aware that things are changing rapidly and that there is much that it does not know. Because issues of fact and value are in a state of flux, it has tended to offer narrow, case-specific rulings that offer little guidance, and constraint, for the future.[9]

But the free-speech principle has an independent life outside of the courtroom. It is often invoked, sometimes strategically though sometimes as a matter of principle, in such a way as to discourage government initiatives that might make the communications market serve democratic goals. Outside of the law, and inside the offices of lobbyists, newspapers, radio stations, and recording studios, as well as even in ordinary

170

households, the First Amendment has a large *cultural* presence. This is no less important than its technical role in courts. Here the identification of the free-speech principle with consumer sovereignty is becoming all the tighter. Worst of all, the emerging cultural understanding severs the link between the First Amendment and democratic self-rule.

Recall here Bill Gates's words: "It's already getting a little unwieldy. When you turn on DirectTV and you step through every channel—well, there's three minutes of your life. When you walk into your living room six years from now, you'll be able to just say what you're interested in, and have the screen help you pick out a video that you care about. It's not going to be 'Let's look at channels 4, 5, and 7.'" Taken to its logical extreme, the emerging wisdom would identify the First Amendment with the dream of unlimited consumer sovereignty with respect to speech. It would see the First Amendment in precisely Gates's terms. It would transform the First Amendment into a constitutional guarantee of consumer sovereignty in the domain of communications.

I have had some experience with the conception of the First Amendment as an embodiment of consumer sovereignty, and it may be useful to offer a brief account of that experience. From 1997 to 1998, I served on the President's Advisory Committee on the Public Interest Obligations of Digital Television Broadcasters. Our task was to consider whether and how television broadcasters should be required to promote public-interest goals—through, for example, closed captioning for the hearing-impaired, emergency warnings, educational programming for children, and free air time for candidates. About half of the committee's members were broadcasters, and most of them were entirely happy to challenge proposed government regulation as intrusive and indefensible. One of the two co-chairs was the redoubtable Leslie

171

Moonves, president of CBS. Moonves is an obviously intelligent, public-spirited man but also the furthest thing from a shrinking violet, and he is, to say the least, attuned to the economic interests of the television networks. Because of its composition, this group was not about to recommend anything dramatic. On the contrary, it was bound to be highly respectful of the prerogatives of television broadcasters. In any case the Advisory Committee was just that—an advisory committee—and we had power only to write a report, and no authority to impose any duties on anyone at all.

Nonetheless, the committee was subject to a sustained, intense, high-profile, and evidently well-funded lobbying effort by economic interests, generally associated with the broadcasting industry, seeking to invoke the First Amendment to suggest that any and all public-interest obligations should and would be found unconstitutional. An elegantly dressed and high-priced Washington lawyer testified before us for an endless hour, making quite outlandish claims about the meaning of the First Amendment. A long stream of legal documents was generated and sent to all of us, most of them arguing that (for example) a requirement of free air time for candidates would offend the Constitution. At our meetings, the most obvious (omni)presence was Jack Goodman, the lawyer for the National Association of Broadcasters (NAB), the lobbying and litigating arm of the broadcast industry, which wields the First Amendment as a kind of protectionist weapon against almost everything that government tries to do. To say that Goodman and the NAB would invoke the free-speech principle at the drop of a hat, or the faintest step of a Federal Communications Commission official in the distance, is only a slight exaggeration.

Of course all this was an entirely legitimate exercise of free speech. But when the President's Advisory Committee on the

Public Interest Obligations of Digital Television Broadcasters already consists, in large part, of broadcasters, and when that very committee is besieged with tendentious and implausible interpretations of the First Amendment, something does seem amiss. There is a more general point. The National Association of Broadcasters and others with similar economic interests typically use the First Amendment in precisely the same way that the National Rifle Association uses the Second Amendment. We should think of the two camps as jurisprudential twins. The National Association of Broadcasters is prepared to make self-serving and outlandish claims about the First Amendment before the public and before courts, and to pay lawyers and publicists a lot of money to help establish those claims. (Perhaps they will ultimately succeed.) The National Rifle Association does the same thing with the Second Amendment. In both cases, those whose social and economic interests are at stake are prepared to use the Constitution, however implausibly invoked, in order to give a veneer of principle and respectability to arguments that would otherwise seem hopelessly partisan and self-interested.

Indeed our advisory committee heard a great deal about the First Amendment, and about marginally relevant Supreme Court decisions, and about footnotes in lower-court opinions, but exceedingly little, in fact close to nothing, about the pragmatic and empirical issues on which many of our inquiries should have turned. If educational programming for children is required on CBS, NBC, and ABC, how many children will end up watching? What would they watch, or do, instead? Would educational programming help them? When educational programming is required, how much do the networks lose in dollars, and who pays the tab—advertisers, consumers, network employees, or someone else? What would be the real-world effects, on citizens and fund-raising alike, of free

173

air time for candidates? Would such a requirement produce more substantial attention to serious issues? Would it reduce current pressures to raise money? What are the consequences of violence on television for both children and adults? Does television violence actually increase violence in the real world? Does it make children anxious in a way that creates genuine psychological harm? How, exactly, are the hard-of-hearing affected when captions are absent?

We can go further still. In the early part of the twentieth century, the due process clause of the Fourteenth Amendment was used to forbid government from regulating the labor market through, for example, minimum-wage and maximum-hour legislation.[10] The Court thought that the Constitution allowed workers and employers to set wages and hours as they "choose," without regulatory constraints. This is one of the most notorious periods in the entire history of the Supreme Court. Judicial use of the Fourteenth Amendment for these purposes is now almost universally agreed to have been a grotesque abuse of power. Nearly everyone now sees that the underlying questions were democratic ones, not ones for the judiciary. The Court should not have forbidden democratic experimentation that would, plausibly at least, have done considerable good.

In fact a central animating idea, in these now-discredited decisions, was that of consumer sovereignty—ensuring that government would not "interfere" with the terms produced by workers, employers, and consumers. (The word "interfere" has to be in quotation marks because the government was there already; the law of property, contract, and torts helps account for how much workers receive, how long they work, and how much consumers pay.) But in the early part of the twenty-first century, the First Amendment is serving a similar purpose in popular debate and sometimes in courts as well.

All too often, it is being invoked on behalf of consumer sovereignty in a way that prevents the democratic process from resolving complex questions that turn on issues of fact and value that are ill-suited to judicial resolution.

To say this is not to say that the First Amendment should play no role at all. On the contrary, it imposes serious limits on what might be done. But some imaginable initiatives, responding to the problems I have discussed thus far, are fully consistent with the free-speech guarantee. Indeed, they would promote its highest aspirations.

Free Speech Is Not an Absolute

We can identify some flaws in the emerging view of the First Amendment by investigating the idea that the free-speech guarantee is "an absolute" in the specific sense that government may not regulate speech at all. This view plays a large role in public debate, and in some ways it is a salutary myth. Certainly the idea that the First Amendment is an absolute helps to discourage government from doing things that it ought not to do. At the same time it gives greater rhetorical power to critics of illegitimate government censorship. But a myth, even if in some ways salutary, remains a myth; and any publicly influential myth is likely to create many problems.

There should be no ambiguity on the point: free speech is not an absolute. We have seen that the government is allowed to regulate speech by imposing neutral rules of property law, telling would-be speakers that they may not have access to certain speech outlets. But this is only the beginning. Government is permitted to regulate computer viruses; unlicensed medical advice; attempted bribery; perjury; criminal conspiracies ("let's fix prices!"); threats to assassinate the president;

175

blackmail ("I'll tell everyone the truth about your private life unless you give me $100"); criminal solicitation ("might you help me rob this bank?"); child pornography; violations of the copyright law; false advertising; purely verbal fraud ("this stock is worth $100,000"); and much more. Many of these forms of speech will not be especially harmful. A fruitless and doomed attempt to solicit someone to commit a crime, for example, is still criminal solicitation; a pitifully executed attempt at fraud is still fraud; sending a computer virus that doesn't actually work is still against the law.

Perhaps you disagree with the view, settled as a matter of current American law (and so settled in most other nations as well), that *all* of these forms of speech are unprotected by the free-speech principle. There is certainly a good argument that some current uses of the copyright law impose unnecessary and unjustifiable restrictions on free speech—and that these restrictions are especially troublesome in the era of the Internet.[11] But you are not a free-speech absolutist unless you believe that *each* of these forms of speech should be protected by that principle. And if this is your belief, you are a most unusual person (and you will have a lot of explaining to do).

This is not the place for a full account of the reach of the First Amendment of the American Constitution.[12] But it is plain that some distinctions must be made among different kinds of speech. It is important, for example, to distinguish between speech that can be shown to be quite harmful and speech that is relatively harmless. As a general rule, the government should not be able to regulate the latter. We might also distinguish between speech that bears on democratic self-government and speech that does not; certainly an especially severe burden should be placed on any government efforts to regulate political speech. Less simply, we might want to distinguish among the *kinds of lines* that government is drawing in terms of the likelihood that government is acting on the basis of illegitimate reasons (a point to which I will return).

These ideas could be combined in various ways, and indeed the fabric of modern free-speech law in America reflects one such combination. Despite the increasing prominence of the idea that the free-speech principle requires unrestricted choices by individual consumers, the Court continues to say that political speech receives the highest protection and that government may regulate (for example) commercial advertising, obscenity, and libel of ordinary people without meeting the especially stringent burden of justification required for political speech. But for present purposes, all that is necessary is to say that no one really believes that the free-speech principle, or the First Amendment, is an absolute. We should be very thankful for that.

The First Amendment and Democratic Deliberation

The fundamental concern of this book is to see how unlimited consumer options might compromise the preconditions of a system of freedom of expression, which include unchosen exposures and shared experiences. To understand the nature of this concern, we will make most progress if we insist that the free-speech principle should be read in light of the commitment to democratic deliberation. In other words, a central point of the free-speech principle is to carry out that commitment.

There are profound differences between those who emphasize consumer sovereignty and those who stress the democratic roots of the free-speech principle. For the latter, government efforts to regulate commercial advertising need not be objectionable. Certainly false and misleading commercial advertising is more readily subject to government control than false and misleading political speech. For those who believe that the free-speech principle has democratic foundations and is not fundamentally about consumer sovereignty, government regulation of television, radio, and the Internet is not always objectionable, at least so long as it is reasonably taken as an effort to promote democratic goals.

Suppose, for example, that government proposes to require television broadcasters (as indeed it now does) to provide three hours per week of educational programming for children. Or suppose that government decides to require television broadcasters to provide a certain amount of free air time for candidates for public office, or a certain amount of time on coverage of elections. For those who believe in consumer sovereignty, these requirements are quite troublesome, indeed they seem like a core violation of the free-speech guarantee. For those who associate the free-speech principle with democratic goals, these requirements are fully consistent with its highest aspirations. Indeed in many democracies—including, for example, Germany and Italy—it is well understood that the mass media can be regulated in the interest of improving democratic self-government.[13]

There is nothing novel or iconoclastic in the democratic conception of free speech. On the contrary, this conception lay at the heart of the original understanding of freedom of speech in America. In attacking the Alien and Sedition Acts, for example, James Madison claimed that they were inconsistent with the free-speech principle, which he linked explicitly to the American transformation of the concept of political sovereignty. In England, Madison noted, sovereignty was vested in the King. But "in the United States, the case is altogether different. The People, not the Government, possess the absolute sovereignty." It was on this foundation that any "Sedition Act" must be judged illegitimate. "[T]he right of electing the members of the Government constitutes . . . the essence of a free and responsible government," and "the value and efficacy of this right depends on the knowledge of the comparative merits and demerits of the candidates for the public trust."[14] It was for this reason that the power represented by a Sedition Act ought, "more than any other, to produce universal alarm; because it is levelled against that right of freely examining public characters and measures, and of free communication among the people thereon, which has ever been justly deemed the only effectual guardian of every other right."

In this way Madison saw "free communication among the people" not as an exercise in consumer sovereignty, in which speech was treated as a kind of commodity, but instead as a central part of self-government, the "only effectual guardian of every other right." Here Madison's conception of free speech was a close cousin of that of Justice Louis Brandeis, who, as we saw in chapter 2, saw public discussion as a "political duty" and believed that the greatest menace to liberty would be "an inert people." A central part of the American constitutional tradition, then, places a high premium on speech that is critical to democratic processes, and centers the First Amendment on the goal of self-government. If history is our guide, it follows that government efforts to promote a well-functioning system of free expression, as through extensions of the public-forum idea, may well be acceptable. It also follows that government faces special burdens when it attempts to regulate political speech, burdens that are somewhat more severe than those it faces when it attempts to regulate other forms of speech.

179

American history is not the only basis for seeing the First Amendment in light of the commitment to democratic deliberation. The argument can be justified by basic principle as well.[15]

Consider the question whether the free-speech principle should be taken to forbid efforts to make communications markets work better from the democratic point of view. Return to our standard examples: educational programming for children, free air time for candidates for public office, closed-captioning for the hearing-impaired. (I am putting the Internet to one side for now because it raises distinctive questions.) Perhaps some of these proposals would do little or no good, or even harm; but from what standpoint should they be judged inconsistent with the free-speech guarantee?

If we believe that the Constitution gives all owners of speech outlets an unbridgeable right to decide what appears on "their" outlets, the answer is clear: government could require none of these things. But why should we believe that? If government is not favoring any point of view, and if it is really improving the operation of democratic processes, it is hard to find a legitimate basis for complaint. Indeed, the Supreme Court has expressly held that the owner of shopping centers—areas where a great deal of speech occurs—may be required to keep their property open for expressive activity.[16] Shopping centers are not television broadcasters; but if a democratic government is attempting to build on the idea of a public forum so as to increase the likelihood of exposure to and debate about diverse views, is there really a reasonable objection from the standpoint of free speech itself?

In a similar vein, it makes sense to say that speech that is political in character, in the sense that it relates to democratic self-government, cannot be regulated without an especially strong showing of government justification—and that commercial advertising, obscenity, and other speech that is not political in that sense can be regulated on the basis of a somewhat weaker government justification. I will not attempt here to offer a full defense of this idea, which of course raises some hard line-drawing problems. But in light of the importance of the question to imaginable government regulation of new technologies, there are three points that deserve brief mention.

First, an insistence that government's burden is greatest when it is regulating political speech emerges from a sensible understanding of government's own incentives. It is here that government is most likely to be acting on the basis of illegitimate considerations, such as self-protection, or giving assistance to powerful private groups. Government is least trustworthy when it is attempting to control speech that might harm its own interests; and when speech is political, government's own interests are almost certainly at stake. This is not to deny that government is often untrustworthy when it is regulating commercial speech, art, or other speech that does not relate to democratic self-government. But we have the strongest reasons to distrust government regulation when political issues are involved.

Second, an emphasis on democratic deliberation protects speech not only when regulation is most likely to be biased, but also when regulation is most likely to be harmful. If government regulates child pornography on the Internet or requires educational programming for children on television, it remains possible to invoke the normal democratic channels to protest these forms of regulation as ineffectual, intrusive, or worse. But when government forbids criticism of an ongoing war effort, the normal channels are foreclosed, in an important sense, by the very regulation at issue. Controls on public debate are uniquely damaging because they impair

181

the process of deliberation that is a precondition for political legitimacy.

Third, an emphasis on democratic deliberation is likely to fit, far better than any alternative, with the most reasonable views about particular free-speech problems. However much we disagree about the most difficult speech problems, we are likely to believe that at a minimum, the free-speech principle protects political expression unless government has exceedingly strong grounds for regulating it. On the other hand, forms of speech such as perjury, attempted bribery, threats, unlicensed medical advice, and criminal solicitation are not likely to seem to be at the heart of the free-speech guarantee.

An understanding of this kind certainly does not answer all constitutional questions. It does not provide a clear test for distinguishing between political and nonpolitical speech, a predictably vexing question.[17] (To those who believe that the absence of a clear test is decisive against the distinction itself, the best response is that any alternative test will lead to line-drawing problems of its own. Because everyone agrees that some forms of speech are regulable, line drawing is literally inevitable. If you're skeptical, try to think of a test that eliminates problems of this kind.) It does not say whether and when government may regulate art or literature, sexually explicit speech, or libelous speech. In all cases, government is required to have a strong justification for regulating speech, political or not. But the approach I am defending does help to orient inquiry. When government is regulating false or fraudulent commercial advertising, libel of private persons, or child pornography, it is likely to be on firm ground. When government is attempting to control criminal conspiracy or speech that contains direct threats of violence aimed at particular people, it need not meet the stringent standards required for regulation of political dissent. What I have suggested here, without fully defending the point, is that a conception of the First Amendment that is rooted in democratic deliberation is an exceedingly good place to start.

Forms of Neutrality

None of this means that the government is permitted to regulate the emerging communications market however it wishes. To know whether to object to what government is doing, it is important to know what *kind* of line it is drawing.[18] There are three possibilities here.

- The government might be regulating speech in a way that is *neutral with respect to the content of the speech at issue*. This is the least objectionable way of regulating speech. For example, government is permitted to say that people may not use loudspeakers on the public streets after midnight or that speakers cannot have access to the front lawn immediately in front of the White House. A regulation of this kind imposes no controls on speech of any particular content. An Internet example: if government says that no one may use the website of CNN unless CNN gives permission, it is acting in a way that is entirely neutral with respect to speech content. So too with restrictions on sending computer viruses. The government bans the ILOVEYOU virus, but it also bans the IHATEYOU virus and the IAMINDIFFEREN-TTOYOU virus. What is against the law is sending viruses; their content is irrelevant.
- The government might regulate speech in a way that depends on the content of what is said, but without discriminating against any particular point of view. Sup-

183

pose, for example, that government bans commercial speech on the subways but allows all other forms of speech on the subways. In the technical language of First Amendment law, this form of regulation is "content-based" but "viewpoint-neutral." Consider the old fairness doctrine, which required broadcasters to cover public issues and to allow speech by those with opposing views. Here the content of speech is highly relevant to what government is requiring, but no specific point of view is benefited or punished. The same can be said for the damages award against the Nuremburg Trials website; the content of the speech definitely mattered, but no particular point of view was being punished. The same award would be given against a website that treated pro-life people in the same way that the Nuremburg Trials treated doctors. In the same category would be a regulation saying that in certain areas, sexually explicit speech must be made inaccessible to children. In these cases, no lines are being drawn directly on the basis of point of view.

• The government might regulate a point of view that it fears or dislikes. This form of regulation is often called "viewpoint discrimination." Government might say, for example, that no one may criticize a decision to go to war, or that no one may claim that one racial group is inferior to another, or that no one may advocate violent overthrow of government. Here the government is singling out a point of view that it wants to ban, perhaps because it believes that the particular point of view is especially dangerous.

It makes sense to say that these three kinds of regulations should be treated differently, on the Internet as elsewhere.

Viewpoint discrimination is the most objectionable. Content-neutral regulation is the least objectionable. If officials are regulating speech because of the point of view that it contains, their action is almost certainly unconstitutional. Government should not be allowed to censor arguments and positions merely because it fears or disapproves of them. If officials are banning a disfavored viewpoint, they ought to be required to show, at the very least, that the viewpoint really creates serious risks that cannot be adequately combated with more speech. Officials ought also be required to explain, in altogether convincing terms, why they are punishing one point of view and not its opposite.

A content-neutral regulation is at the opposite extreme, and such regulations are often legitimate. If the government has acted in a content-neutral way, courts usually do not and should not intervene, at least if the basic channels of communications remain open, and if government has a solid reason for the regulation. Of course a gratuitous or purposeless regulation must be struck down even if it is content-neutral. Suppose that government says that the public streets—or for that matter the Internet—may be used for expressive activity, but only between 8 p.m. and 8:30 p.m. If so, the neutrality of the regulation is no defense. But content-neutral regulations are frequently easy to justify; their very neutrality, and hence breadth, ensures that there is a good reason for them. The government is unlikely to ban expressive activity from 8:30 p.m. until 7:59 a.m. because so many people would resist the ban. The more likely regulation prohibits noisy demonstrations when people are trying to sleep, and there is nothing wrong with such prohibitions.

Now consider the intermediate case. When government is regulating in a way that is based on content but neutral with respect to point of view, there are two issues. The first is

185

whether the particular line being drawn suggests lurking viewpoint discrimination—a hidden but detectable desire to ban a certain point of view. When it does, the law should probably be struck down. If government says that the most recent war, or abortion, may not be discussed on television, it is, as a technical matter, discriminating against a whole topic, not against any particular point of view; but there is pretty good reason to suspect government's motivations. A ban on discussion of the most recent war is probably an effort to protect the government from criticism.

The second and perhaps more fundamental issue is whether government is able to invoke strong, content-neutral grounds for engaging in this form of regulation. A ban on televised discussion of the most recent war should be struck down for this reason. The ban seems to have no real point, aside from forbidding certain points of view from being expressed. But the government has a stronger argument if, for example, it is requiring broadcasters to offer three hours of educational programming for children. In that case, it is trying to ensure that television serves children, an entirely legitimate interest.

Of course some cases may test the line between discrimination on the basis of content and discrimination on the basis of viewpoint. If government is regulating sexually explicit speech when that speech offends contemporary community standards, is it regulating on the basis of viewpoint or merely content? This is not an easy question, and many people have argued over the right answer. But an understanding of the three categories discussed here should be sufficient to make sense out of the bulk of imaginable free-speech challenges— and should provide some help in approaching the rest of them as well.

186

Penalties and Subsidies

Of course government can do a range of things to improve the system of free speech. Here it is important to make a further distinction, between "subsidies" on the one hand and "penalties" on the other. Government is likely to have a great deal of trouble when it is imposing penalties on speech. Such penalties are the model of what a system of free expression avoids. Government will have more room to maneuver if it is giving out selective subsidies. Public officials are not required to give money out to all speakers, and if they are giving money to some people but not to others, they may well be on firm ground. But the distinction between the penalties and subsidies is not always obvious.

The most conspicuous penalties are criminal and civil punishments. If government makes it a crime to libel people over the Internet or imposes civil fines on television broadcasters who do not provide free air time for candidates for office, it is punishing speech. The analysis of these penalties should depend on the considerations discussed thus far—whether political speech is involved, what kind of line the government is drawing, and so forth.

Somewhat trickier, but belonging in the same category, are cases in which government is *withdrawing a benefit to which people would otherwise be entitled* when the reason for the withdrawal is the government's view about the appropriate content of speech. Suppose, for example, that government gives an annual cash subsidy to all speakers of a certain kind—say, those networks that agree to provide educational programming for children. But suppose that government withdraws the subsidy from those networks that provide speech of which the government disapproves. Imagine, for

187

example, that the government withdraws the subsidy from networks whose news shows are critical of the president. For the most part, these sorts of penalties should be analyzed in exactly the same way as criminal or civil punishment. When benefits are being withdrawn, just as when ordinary punishment is being imposed, government is depriving people of goods to which they would otherwise be entitled, and we probably have excellent reason to distrust its motives. If government responds to dissenters by taking away benefits that they would otherwise receive, it is violating the free-speech principle.

But a quite different issue is posed when government gives out selective subsidies to speakers. It often does this by, for example, funding some museums and artists but not others, and generally through the National Endowment for the Arts and the Public Broadcasting System. Imagine a situation in which government is willing to fund educational programming for children and pays a station to air that programming on Saturday morning—without also funding situation comedies or game shows. Or imagine that government funds a series of historical exhibits on the Civil War without also funding exhibits on the Vietnam War, or on World War II, or on the history of sex equality in America. What is most important here can be stated very simply: *under current law in the United States (and generally elsewhere), government is permitted to subsidize speech however it wishes.*[19]

Government often *is* a speaker, and as such, it is permitted to say whatever it likes. No one thinks that there is a problem if officials endorse one view and reject another. And if government seeks to use taxpayer funds to subsidize certain projects and enterprises, there is usually no basis for constitutional complaint. The only exception to this principle is that if government is allocating funds to private speakers in a way that discriminates on the basis of viewpoint, there might be a First Amendment problem.[20] The precise nature of this exception remains unclear. But it would certainly be possible to challenge, on constitutional grounds, a decision by government to fund the Republican Party website without also funding the Democratic Party website.

Of course this kind of discrimination goes far beyond anything that I shall be suggesting here. What is important, then, is that government has a great deal of room to maneuver insofar as it is not penalizing speech but instead subsidizing it.

A Restrained, Prudent First Amendment

This chapter has dealt with a range of free-speech issues, some of them briskly, and it is important not to lose the forest for the trees. My basic claims have been that the First Amendment in large part embodies a democratic ideal, that it should not be identified with the notion of consumer sovereignty, and that it is not an absolute. The core requirement of the free-speech principle is that with respect to politics, government must remain neutral among points of view. Content regulation is disfavored; viewpoint discrimination is almost always out of bounds. A key task is to ensure compliance with these requirements in the contemporary environment.

9

Policies and Proposals

THERE IS a large difference between consumers and citizens, and a well-functioning democratic order would be compromised by a fragmented system of communications. Having urged these points, I do not intend to offer any kind of blueprint for the future; this is not a policy manual. Recall too that some problems lack solutions. But surely things can be made better rather than worse. In thinking about what might be done by either private or public institutions, it is important to have some sense of the problems that we aim to address, and of some possible ways of addressing them.

If the discussion thus far is correct, there are three fundamental concerns from the democratic point of view. These include:

- the need for attention to substantive questions of policy and principle, combined with a range of positions on such questions;
- the value of exposure to materials, topics, and positions that people would not have chosen in advance, or at least enough exposure to produce a degree of understanding and curiosity; and
- the importance of a range of common experiences.

Of course it would be ideal if citizens were demanding, and private providers were creating, a range of initiatives designed to alleviate the underlying concerns. To some extent, they are; exceedingly promising experiments have been emerging in just this vein. Our emphasis should be on purely private solutions through a better understanding of what is entailed by the notion of citizenship. The Internet and other communications technologies create extraordinary and ever-growing opportunities for exposure to diverse points of view, and indeed increased opportunities for shared experiences and substantive discussions of both policy and principle. It is certainly possible that private choices will lead to far more, not less, in the way of exposure to new topics and viewpoints, and also to more, not less, in the way of shared experiences. But to the extent that they fail to do so, it is worthwhile to consider how self-conscious efforts by private institutions, and to some extent public ones as well, might pick up the slack.

Any ideas about how to handle the situation require an understanding of how people are likely to react to topics and points of view that they have not chosen. If people cannot develop an interest in topics that they would not have chosen, then exposure to those topics is unlikely to be worthwhile. If people will never listen to points of view with which they disagree, there would be little point in exposing them to those points of view. If people would never learn from exposure to unchosen views and topics, we might as well build on the emerging capacity of companies to discern and predict tastes and just allow people to see, hear, and get what they already like. Recall collaborative filtering and technology's amazing ability to predict what you'll like—simply by combining information about what you've chosen with information about what people who have chosen what you chose have also chosen.

But it seems far more realistic to say that many people—it would be silly to say exactly how many, but surely millions—are prepared to listen to points of view that they have not se-

191

lected. Many people are fully prepared to develop an interest in topics that they have not selected and in fact know nothing about. To work well, a deliberative democracy had better have many such people. It cannot possibly function without them. And if many people are able to benefit from wider exposure, it is worthwhile to think about ways to improve the communications market to their, and our, advantage.

I briefly discuss several possibilities here, including:

- deliberative domains;
- disclosure of relevant conduct by networks and other large producers of communications;
- voluntary self-regulation;
- economic subsidies, including publicly subsidized programming and websites;
- "must-carry" policies, designed to promote education and attention to public issues;
- the creative use of links to draw people's attention to multiple views.

Of course different proposals would work better for some communications outlets than for others, and I will emphasize these differences here. Disclosure of public-affairs programming is sensible for television and radio broadcasters, but not for websites. I will be exploring "must-carry" requirements for television stations, but with respect to the Internet, such requirements would be hard to justify—and would almost certainly be unconstitutional. I will be arguing for the creative use of links on the Internet, but I will not suggest, and do not believe, that the government should require any links. Most important, the goals of the proposals could be implemented through private action, which is the preferred approach by far.

Deliberative Domains and the Internet

It would be extremely valuable to have several widely publi-
cized deliberative domains on the Internet, ensuring opportunities for discussion among people with diverse views. In
chapter 3, we encountered James Fishkin's deliberative opinion poll, attempting to describe public opinion not after tele-
phone calls to people in their homes for unreflective responses, but as a result of extended discussions in groups of
heterogeneous people. Fishkin has created a website with a
great deal of valuable and fascinating material (see "The Center for Deliberative Democracy," http://cdd.stanford.edu/).
Along with many others, Fishkin has been engaged in a process of creating deliberative opportunities on the Internet—
spaces where people with different views can meet and exchange reasons, and have a chance to understand, at least a
bit, the point of view of those who disagree with them. The
hope is that citizen engagement, mutual understanding, and
better thinking will emerge as a result.

Imagine, a new website: deliberativedemocracy.com—or if
you wish, deliberativedemocracy.org. (Neither name is yet
taken; I've checked.) The site could easily be created by the
private sector. When you come to the site, you might find a
general description of goals and contents. Everyone would
understand that this is a place where people of very different
views are invited to listen and to speak. And once you're
there, you would be able to read and (if you wish) participate
in discussions of a topic of your choice, by clicking on icons
representing, for example, national security, relevant wars,
civil rights, the environment, unemployment, foreign affairs,
poverty, the stock market, children, gun control, labor unions,
and much more. Many of these topics might have icons with

193

smaller subtopics—under environment, for example, there might be discussions of global warming, genetically engineered food, water pollution, and hazardous waste sites. Each topic and subtopic could provide brief descriptions of agreed-upon facts and competing points of view as an introduction and frame for the discussion. Private creativity on the part of users would undoubtedly take things in boundless unanticipated directions. Private managers of such sites would have their own norms about how people should interact with one another; deliberativedemocracy .com, for example, might encourage norms of civility.

Many such experiments are now emerging, sometimes self-consciously, sometimes through the kinds of spontaneous developments that occur on email and listserves. The Deliberative Democracy Consortium is especially noteworthy here: it offers a range of references, links, and materials (see http://www.deliberative-democracy.net/). For obvious reasons, there would be many advantages to a situation in which a few deliberative sites were especially prominent. If this were the case, deliberativedemocracy.com, for example, would have a special salience for many citizens, providing a forum in which hundreds of thousands, or even millions, could participate, if only through occasional reading. But we should hardly be alarmed if a large number of deliberative websites were to emerge and to compete with one another—a plausible description of what is starting to happen.

Perhaps some governments could provide a funding mechanism to subsidize the development of some such sites, without having a managerial role (see below). But what is most important is general awareness of the importance of deliberation to a well-functioning democracy, and of deliberation among people who do not agree. If that awareness is widespread, sites of the sort that I am describing here will grow up and flourish entirely on their own.

Disclosure and Large Providers of Information: Sunlight as Disinfectant

The last decades have seen an extraordinary growth in the use of a simple regulatory tool: the requirement that people disclose what they are doing. In the environmental area, this has been an exceptionally effective strategy. Probably the most striking example is the Emergency Planning and Community Right-to-Know Act (EPCRA). Under this statute, firms and individuals must report to state and local government the quantities of potentially hazardous chemicals that have been stored or released into the environment. This has been an amazing and unanticipated success story: mere disclosure, or threat of disclosure, has resulted in voluntary, low-cost reductions in toxic releases.[1]

It should be no wonder that disclosure has become a popular approach to dealing with pollution. When polluters are required to disclose their actions, political pressures, or market pressures, will lead to reductions, without any need for actual government mandates. Ideally, of course, no requirements need to be imposed. People will disclose on their own, in part because of the public demand for relevant information. In the area of communications, voluntary disclosure should be preferred. But if it is not forthcoming, disclosure requirements might be imposed, certainly on large polluters, and perhaps on television and radio broadcasters too.

Suppose, for example, that certain programming might be harmful to children, and that certain other programming might be beneficial to society. Is there a way to discourage

195

the bad and to encourage the good without regulating speech directly? Disclosure policies suggest a promising possibility, at least if it is possible to specify what is being disclosed. Thus the mandatory "V-Chip" is intended to permit parents to block programming that they want to exclude from their homes; the V-Chip is supposed to work hand in hand with a ratings system giving information about the suitability of programming for children of various ages. Similarly, a provision of the 1996 Telecommunications Act imposes three relevant require- ments. First, television manufacturers must include technol- ogy capable of reading a program-rating mechanism. Second, the FCC must create a ratings methodology if the industry does not produce an acceptable ratings plan within a year. Third, broadcasters must include a rating in their signals if the relevant program is rated. The ratings system has now been in place for many years, and it seems to have been, at the very least, a modest success, making it far simpler and easier for parents to monitor what children are seeing.

A chief advantage of disclosure policies is their comparative flexibility. If viewers know the nature of network policies in advance, they can impose market pressures by watching more or less; broadcasters are of course responsive to those pres- sures. People can also impose political pressures by complain- ing to stations or to elected representatives, and here too it is possible to induce changes. From the democratic point of view, disclosure also has substantial virtues. A well-function- ing system of deliberative democracy requires a certain de- gree of information so that citizens can engage in their moni- toring and deliberative tasks. A good way to enable citizens to oversee private or public action—and also to assess the need for less, more, or different regulation—is to inform them of both private and public activity. The very fact that the public will be in a position to engage in general monitoring may well spur better choices on the part of those who provide television and radio programming.

Disclosure could be used in many different ways, suitable for different communications media. Disclosure policies of various sorts might, for example, be voluntarily adopted by television and radio broadcasters and by cable television stations. The idea here, associated with Justice Louis Brandeis, is that "sunlight is the best of disinfectants." And if such policies are not adopted voluntarily, legal requirements might be considered. The idea would be to ensure that anyone who is engaging in a practice that might produce harm, or do less good than might be done, should be required to disclose that fact to the public.[2] The disclosure might or might not alter behavior. If it does not alter behavior, we have reason to believe that the public is not much concerned about it. If the behavior does change, the public was, in all likelihood, sufficiently exercised to demand it.

As an illustration, consider a simple proposal: *television and radio broadcasters should be required to disclose, in some detail and on a quarterly basis, all of their public-service and public-interest activities.* The disclosure might include an accounting of any free air time provided to candidates, opportunities to speak for those addressing public issues, rights of reply, educational programming, charitable activities, programming designed for traditionally underserved communities, closed captioning for the hearing impaired, local programming, and public-service announcements. Astonishingly, most radio and television broadcasters have yet to disclose this information to the public, though some information gathering has been done by the National Association of Broadcasters. A hope, vindicated by similar approaches in environmental law, is that a disclosure requirement will by itself trigger improved performance by creating a kind of competition to do more and

197

better, and by enlisting various social pressures in the direction of improved performance.

I have referred several times to the old fairness doctrine, which required broadcasters to cover public issues and to allow a right of reply for dissenting views. We have seen that this doctrine was repealed largely on the ground that it chilled coverage of public issues in the first instance. We have also seen that while the repeal was amply justified, it has had a downside insofar as it has increased fragmentation and hence polarization. But whether or not we think the old fairness doctrine was defensible, a disclosure requirement—tied to coverage of public issues and diversity of views—would be a far less intrusive way of accomplishing the most appealing goals of that doctrine. Such a requirement might well produce some movement toward more coverage of public issues and more attention to diverse views. It is even possible that such a requirement would help to address the three problems identified at the beginning of this chapter.

It is also possible that any disclosure requirement would produce no movement at all. But notice that people did not anticipate that the Toxic Release Inventory would by itself spur reductions in toxic releases, as it emphatically did. In order for voluntary improvements to occur, the disclosure requirements must be accompanied by economic or political pressure of some kind, perhaps from external monitors, or at least a degree of conscience on the part of producers. If there are external monitors, and if those monitors are able to impose costs on those with bad records, disclosure is likely to do some good.

The external monitors might include public interest groups seeking to "shame" badly performing broadcasters. They might include rivals who seek to create a kind of "race to the top" in the form of better performance. They might include newspaper reporters and websites. If public-interest organizations and viewers who favor certain programming are able to mobilize, perhaps in concert with certain members of the mass media, substantial improvements might be expected. It is even possible that a disclosure requirement would help create its own monitors. And in view of the relative unintrusiveness of a disclosure requirement, and the flexibility of any private responses, this approach is certainly worth trying. At worst, little will be lost. At most, something will be gained, probably in the form of better programming and greater information about the actual performance of the industry. In light of the aspirations of most viewers, the possible result of disclosure will be to improve the quality and quantity of both educational and civic programming in a way that promotes the goals of a well-functioning deliberative democracy.

My emphasis here has been on the application of disclosure requirements to television and radio broadcasters. But I do not suggest that such requirements should be imposed on websites. In view of their remarkable range and diversity, no such requirements would make sense. What, exactly, would be disclosed by amazon.com, gm.com, startrek.com, bradpittfan.com, foxsports.com, columbia.edu, or republic .com? Of course some disclosures, and some warnings, might be provided voluntarily. For example, many websites already inform people of content unsuitable for children. Other disclosure practices could undoubtedly help both consumers and citizens. But for purposes of my concerns here, those practices should not be compelled.

Voluntary Self-Regulation and Best Practices

A somewhat more ambitious approach, going beyond mere disclosure, would involve voluntary self-regulation by those who provide information. One of the most noteworthy trends of the last two decades, inside and outside the world of communications, has been in the direction of such self-regulation, which is designed to protect a range of social goals.[3] In the area of occupational safety, for example, many employers follow agreed-upon "best practices," designed to reduce the level of accidents and disease. Similar approaches are followed in the environmental area. The same idea might easily be adopted for democratic purposes. Radio stations might agree, perhaps via some kind of code of conduct, to attempt to provide a wide range of views on public issues, so as to ensure that listeners encounter something other than a loud version of what they already think.

One of the motivating ideas behind voluntary self-regulation is that competition among producers, while usually wonderful, can sometimes be harmful from the point of view of the public as a whole.[4] Endless efforts to get people's attention may do long-term damage. Everyone knows that there has been an increasing trend toward "tabloidization," with mainstream newspapers and broadcasters emphasizing scandals and sensationalism. This trend predated the Internet, but it seems to have been accelerated by the Internet. Often the news seems not to involve news at all. Sometimes it seems to be a continuation of the fictional drama that preceded it with detailed discussion of the "real-life events" mirrored in the fiction. Many journalists worry about this problem. As Robert Frank and Phillip Cook warn, with reference to the effects of market forces:[5]

> Increasingly impoverished political debate is yet another cost of our current cultural trajectory. Complex modern societies generate complex economic and social problems, and the task of choosing the best course is difficult under the best of circum-

200

stances. And yet, as in-depth analysis and commentary give way to sound bites in which rival journalists and politicians mercilessly ravage one another, we become an increasingly ill-informed and ill-tempered electorate.

But an agreement among producers can break (or brake) this competition, and hence perform some of the valuable functions of law—without intruding law into the domain of speech regulation.

With respect to television, consider the possibility of promoting democratic goals through voluntary self-regulation, as through a code of conduct to be issued and promoted by the National Association of Broadcasters (NAB), or perhaps by a wider range of those who produce television for the American public. For many decades, in fact, the NAB did administer such a code. It did so partly to promote its economic interests (by raising the price of advertising), partly to fend off regulation (by showing that the industry was engaged in beneficial self-regulation, making government efforts unnecessary), and partly to carry out the moral commitments of broadcasters themselves. Notably, voluntary self-regulation has played a role in numerous areas of media policy, including, for example, cigarette advertising, children's advertising, family viewing, advertising of hard liquor, and fairness in news reporting. In the 1980s, continuing congressional concern about televised violence led to a new law creating an antitrust exemption for networks, broadcasters, cable operators and programmers, and trade associations, precisely in order to permit them to generate standards to reduce the amount of violence on television. As we have seen, a ratings system for television is now in place, and it should be treated as a successful example of voluntary self-regulation, giving parents a general sense of the appropriateness of programming.

201

A new code, adopted by some if not all, might address a number of the problems discussed thus far. For example, signatories could agree to cover substantive issues in a serious way, to avoid sensationalistic treatment of politics, to give extended coverage to public issues, and to allow diverse voices to be heard. In fact ideas of this kind long played a role in the television industry until the abandonment of the broadcasters' code in 1979. In view of the increasing range of options and the declining centrality of television broadcasters, there are undoubtedly limits to how much can be done through this route. But in many contexts voluntary self-regulation of this kind has produced considerable good, and a code of some kind could provide a sort of quality assurance to the public.

If formal codes of conduct are not feasible—and they probably are not—we could imagine less formal efforts to establish and to follow best practices. For providers of television and radio, such practices might deal with programming for children, emergency situations, and perhaps coverage of elections. It is also possible to imagine informal agreements or understandings among some websites, designed to protect children, to ensure privacy, and to promote attention to diverse views. If market forces are producing serious problems, we have every reason to encourage creative thinking in this vein.

Subsidies

An additional possibility, also with an established history, would involve government subsidies. With respect to television and radio, many nations, including the United States, have relied on a combination of private and public funding. In the United States, the Public Broadcasting System (PBS) is designed to provide programming, including educational

202

shows for children, that, it is believed, will find insufficient funding in the private domain. Interestingly, and contrary to common belief, most of PBS's funding comes from private sources; but the government does provide significant help. This is a genuine public-private partnership. And in many domains, taxpayer resources are given to assist those who produce artistic, cultural, and historical works of many different kinds.

The traditional rationale for a separate public broadcasting network has been weakened by the massive proliferation of options, including many, on both television and the Internet, that provide discussion of public issues and educational programming for children. This is not to say that the rationale has been eliminated. Ten of millions of Americans continue to rely on over-the-air broadcasting, and many of them benefit from, and depend on, PBS. Nor do I mean to suggest that in all respects, the situation is better now than it was when the universe of options was so much smaller. In a system with four channels, PBS had a kind of salience that it now lacks, and it is by no means clear that the current situation, with dozens or hundreds of available stations, is in every way an improvement for all children or all adults. Public broadcasting continues to provide important services. But with many private outlets doing the same kind of thing, it does seem clear that the rationale for PBS, in its current form, is weaker than it once was.

What, if anything, might be done in addition or instead? One possibility is to use modest levels of taxpayer money to assist high-quality efforts in nonprofit, nongovernmental spaces on the Internet. Such spaces are now proliferating, and they are adding a great deal to our culture. Of course taxpayer funds are limited and there are claims on government resources with higher priority. My only point it that it is worth rethinking the PBS model. It is past time to consider new initiatives that make better sense in the new communications environment.

"Must Carry": Constitutional Debates

Some of the most interesting developments in the law of speech involve "access rights," or "must-carry" rules. In fact the public-forum doctrine creates a kind of must-carry rule for streets and parks. These sites must be opened up for speech. You and I are entitled to have access to them. Is there any place for must-carry rules on television or radio, or is the whole idea a relic of the past?

To answer these questions, it is necessary to have some sense of the legal background. In the 1970s, the Supreme Court held that government has the authority to subject television and radio broadcasters to a kind of must-carry rule, in the form of the old fairness doctrine, requiring attention to public issues and an opportunity for diverse views to speak.[6] At the same time, the Court firmly rejected the idea that private newspapers may be treated as public forums and subject to must-carry rules.[7] In the Court's view, the government could not force newspapers to give a "right of reply" to those who sought to combat a controversial statement of opinion or fact. The apparent difference between broadcasters and newspapers—fragile even in the 1970s, and fragile to the breaking point today—is that the former are "scarce," largely for technological reasons, and hence are more properly subject to governmental controls.

Now that the scarcity rationale is so much weaker, the continued viability of the fairness doctrine remains an open question. If the FCC tried to reinstate the doctrine, the Court would probably strike it down. But the Court has nonetheless upheld legislation that imposes must-carry rules on cable television providers.[8] The relevant legislation, still on the books, requires cable providers to set aside a number of their channels for both "local commercial television stations" and "noncommercial educational television stations." Congress defended these requirements as a way of ensuring the economic viability of broadcasters, on whom many millions of Americans continue to rely. In finding the must-carry requirements constitutional, the Court said, "assuring that the public has access to a multiplicity of information sources is a governmental purpose of the highest order, for it promotes values central to the First Amendment." The Court also emphasized the "potential for abuse of . . . private power over a central avenue of communication," and stressed that the Constitution "does not disable the government from taking steps to ensure that private interests not restrict, through physical control of a critical pathway of communication, the free flow of information and ideas."

In so saying, the Court was recalling Justice Brandeis's emphatically republican conception of the First Amendment. Indeed, Justice Breyer, in a separate opinion, made the link with Justice Brandeis explicit: the statute's "policy, in turn, seeks to facilitate the public discussion and informed deliberation, which, as Justice Brandeis pointed out many years ago, democratic government presupposes and the First Amendment seeks to achieve."[9] Here, then, is an unambiguous endorsement of the idea that government has the power to regulate communications technologies in order to promote goals associated with deliberative democracy. Justice Breyer's general approach to the Constitution is in this vein: he reads the Constitution as a whole in the terms of deliberative democracy.[10]

205

So far, so good. But for those interested in thinking about the implications of the Court's decision, there is considerable ambiguity in the Court's decision. How crucial was it, to the Court's reasoning, that the cable provider controlled access to cable stations? Suppose that government imposed must-carry rules on cbs.com, cnn.com, or foxnews.com—arguing that one or the other of these must ensure sufficient diversity of view, or cover issues of importance to local communities. We might imagine a law requiring foxnews.com to give more attention to "liberal" positions—or that cnn.com ensure that when New Yorkers click on its site, they see stories that bear on New York in particular. In my view, no such requirements would be sensible, and if they were imposed, they should be struck down (quickly) as unconstitutional. The sheer range of views on the Internet would make it impermissibly selective to single out foxnews.com for special obligations; and a general requirement, imposed on all sites, would be far too intrusive to be justifiable. Coverage of local issues is important, but the massive increase in options means that such coverage is readily available. It may take a few seconds to find it, but is that a serious problem?

"Must carry" has no legitimate role on the Internet. Of course it remains true that providers, including cnn.com and foxnews.com, do best if they give sympathetic and substantive attention to a number of views, not only one.

Links, Icons, Blogrolls, and the Scarce Commodity of Attention

I have emphasized that one of the most important of all commodities in the current situation is people's attention. This is what companies are endlessly competing to obtain. Much activity on the Internet by those interested in profits and other goods is designed to produce greater attention, even if only for a moment. If a company, or a political candidate, can get attention from 300,000 people for as little as two seconds, it will have accomplished a great deal.

Almost everyone has noticed that many Internet sites do not, and need not, charge a fee for users. If you want to go to WashingtonPost.com or Latimes.com, you can read everything for free, and you can get the content of countless other magazines and newspapers without paying a penny. (The *New York Times* charges a small amount for some of its articles; the same is true for the *New Republic*.) Nor is the phenomenon limited to magazines and newspapers. If you want to learn about cancer, you can find out a great deal from plwc.com, entirely free of charge. Google.com charges nothing for its search service. Why is this? In most of these cases, advertisers are willing to foot the bill. What advertisers are buying is access, and usually brief access at that, to people's eyes—a small period of attention.

Here again we can see that those who use websites are commodities at least as much as they are consumers. They are what websites are selling to advertisers for a fee, sometimes a large one. Targeting and customization are playing a large role here, as advertisers come to learn, with some precision, how many people, and which people, "visit" from which advertisements. Of course advertisements cannot guarantee sales. Most people who see an icon for Bloomingdales.com, Amazon.com, or Netflix.com will simply ignore it. But some will not; they will be curious and see what there is to see. Or they will file it away in some part of their minds for future use.

If we combine an understanding of access rights and must-carry rules with an appreciation of the crucial role of attention, we might enlist advertisers' practices in the service of public-interest goals. In other words, public-spirited actors, knowing that attention is valuable, might think of ways to capture that attention, not to coerce people, but to trigger their interest in material that might produce individual and social benefits. Icons that represent links among sites are the obvious strategy here; I am focusing on voluntary linking decisions, not on government mandates.

In the context of the Internet, the point of links is to get people's attention, however fleetingly. Consider in this light a proposal: providers of material with a certain point of view might also provide links to sites with a very different point of view. The *Nation*, a liberal magazine whose site features left-of-center opinions, might agree to provide icons for the *Weekly Standard*, a conservative magazine, in return for an informal agreement from the *Weekly Standard* to provide icons for the *Nation*. The icon itself would not require anyone to read anything. It would merely provide a signal, to the viewer, that there is a place where a different point of view might be consulted. Of the thousands or millions of people who choose any particular site, not most, but undoubtedly a few, would be sufficiently interested to look further. Best of all, this form of "carriage" would replicate many features of the public street and the general-interest intermediary. It would alert people to the existence of materials other than those which they usually read. We have seen that some sites do this already. The problem is that the practice remains unusual.

We could even foresee a situation in which many partisan sites offer links implicitly saying something like this: "We have a clear point of view, and we hope that more people will come to believe what we do. But we are also committed to democratic debate and to discussion among people who think

208

differently. To that end we are providing links to other sites, in the interest of providing genuine debate on these issues." If many sites would agree to do this, the problem of fragmentation would be reduced.

Even now, textual references to organizations or institutions are often hyperlinks, so that when a magazine such as the *National Review* refers to the World Wildlife Fund, or Environmental Defense, it also allows readers instant access to their sites. As compared with icons, the advantage of the hyperlink approach is that it is less trouble for the owner and less intrusive on the owner's prerogatives—indeed, it is barely an intrusion at all. In chapter 3 we saw that it is common for political sites to offer links to like-minded sites, but quite uncommon for them to offer links to those with opposed views. We could easily imagine the emergence of a new and good democratic custom: sites would generally ensure that references to other organizations are hyperlinks too. To some extent, of course, this is already the norm.

In a similar vein, public-spirited bloggers would do well to offer links to those whose views are quite different from their own. Liberal blogs could more regularly link to conservative ones, and vice versa. Many bloggers offer "blogrolls" in which they list other blogs that they like or otherwise seek to publicize. As it turns out, liberal bloggers seem to list mostly or only liberal bloggers on their blogrolls, and conservative bloggers show the same pattern. It would be good to show greater diversity, through a norm by which both liberals and conservatives include at least a few high-quality blogs from people with whom they do not agree. We could easily imagine explicit or implicit "deals" among bloggers with competing opinions, producing mutual linking. Such deals would increase the likelihood that people would be exposed to differ-

209

ent perspectives; they would also reflect a healthy degree of mutual respect.

I do not suggest or believe that government should require anything of this kind. Some constitutional questions are hard, but this one is easy: any such requirements would violate the First Amendment. If site owners and bloggers do not want to provide icons or links, they are entitled to refuse to do so. What is most important is that we could easily imagine a situation in which icons and links are more standard practices, in a way that would promote the goals of both consumers and citizens, and do so without compromising the legitimate interests of site owners.

The Tyranny of the Status Quo

The tyranny of the status quo has many sources. Sometimes it is based on a fear of unintended consequences, as in the economists' plea, "the perfect is the enemy of the good"—a mantra of resignation to which we should respond, with John Dewey, that "the better is the enemy of the still better." Sometimes it is grounded in a belief, widespread though palpably false, that things cannot be different from what they now are. (Things were different yesterday, and they will be different tomorrow.) Sometimes proposed changes seem to be hopelessly utopian, far too much so to be realistic. And sometimes they seem small and incremental, even silly, and to do nothing large enough to solve the underlying problems.

The suggestions I have offered here are modest and incremental. They are designed to give some glimpses of the possibilities, and also to do at least a little bit of good. Some of them merely build on existing practices. What is especially important in the current era is that we retain a sense of the grounds on which we can evaluate them. To those skeptical of the proposals outlined here, it makes sense to ask: If we seek to enlist current technologies in the service of democratic ideals, what kinds of practices would be better?

10

Republic.com

MUCH OF what I have argued here is captured in some passages from two great theorists of freedom and democracy, John Stuart Mill and John Dewey. First, Mill:

> It is hardly possible to overstate the value, in the present low state of human improvement, of placing human beings in contact with other persons dissimilar to themselves, and with modes of thought and action unlike those with which they are familiar. . . . Such communication has always been, and is peculiarly in the present age, one of the primary sources of progress.[1]

And now Dewey:

> The belief that thought and its communication are now free simply because legal restrictions which once obtained have been done away is absurd. Its currency perpetuates the infantile state of social knowledge. For it blurs recognition of our central need to possess conceptions which are used as tools of directed inquiry and which are tested, rectified and caused to grow in actual use. No man and no mind was ever emancipated merely by being left alone.[2]

With these ideas in view, I have stressed the serious problems, for individuals and societies alike, that are likely to be created by the practice of self-insulation—by a situation in which many of us wall ourselves off from the concerns and opinions of our fellow citizens. The ideal of consumer sovereignty, well-represented in the supposedly utopian vision of complete "personalization," would undermine democratic ideals. Rather than a utopian vision, the Daily Me is best understood as a kind of nightmare, the stuff of science fiction, carrying large lessons about some neglected requirements of democratic self-government.

Within and Without Enclaves

A fully personalized speech market, consisting of countless niches, would make self-government less workable. In important ways it would reduce, not increase, freedom for the individuals involved. It would create a high degree of social fragmentation. It would make mutual understanding far more difficult among individuals and groups. To the extent that people are using the Internet in this way, they are disserving themselves and their fellow citizens.

I do not mean to say that this is the usual pattern or that this is what most people are mostly doing. Many people are sufficiently curious to use new technologies to see a wide range of topics and views. Millions of people now do exactly that. The current picture shows that general-interest intermediaries continue to have a large role. As we have seen, the Internet's public sphere is networked. But clustering is nonetheless common, and group polarization is a significant risk even if only a relatively small proportion of people chooses to listen and speak with those who are like-minded. A free society benefits from public domains offering a wide variety of topics and positions.

Nothing in these claims is inconsistent with the view that a free society also makes spaces for freedom of choice and for deliberating enclaves consisting of like-minded individuals. It should not be necessary to emphasize that freedom of choice is an individual and social good. Moreover, deliberating enclaves ensure that positions that would otherwise be silenced or squelched have a chance to develop. Individual members of such groups sometimes have a hard time communicating their views to the wider society, and if group members can speak among themselves, they can learn a great deal and ultimately contribute much more to their discussions with others. Recall the importance of "second-order diversity"—the kind of diversity that comes when society benefits from many groups with clear practices and positions of their own.[3] If a nation allows many organizations to exist, and if each of them is fairly uniform, the nation may well benefit from the great range of views that will emerge.

Although I have suggested that group polarization and local cascades present serious dangers, similar phenomena played an unquestionable role in movements that have and deserve widespread approval. To take just a few examples, consider the attack on apartheid in South Africa, the civil rights movement in the United States, the assault on slavery itself. Nor are group polarization and local cascades merely a matter of historical interest. Consider, for example, private conversations among political dissenters of various kinds, cancer patients, science fiction enthusiasts, those concerned about avian flu, parents of children with physical or mental disabilities, poor tenants, and members of religious minorities. Insofar as new technologies make it easier to construct enclaves for communication among people with common experiences and complaints, they are a boon as well as a danger. Internet discussion groups, for example, can allow people to discuss shared difficulties when they would otherwise feel quite isolated and think, wrongly, that their condition is unique or in any case hopeless. This is highly desirable for the people involved and also for society as a whole.

The danger of deliberating enclaves should by now be familiar. Their members may move to positions that lack merit but are predictable consequences of the particular pressures produced by deliberation among the like-minded. In the extreme case, enclave deliberation may even put social stability at risk (sometimes for better, usually for worse). Terrorism is itself a product of deliberation among like-minded people. I have suggested that extremists often suffer from a kind of "crippled epistemology," in the form of exposure to a small subset of relevant information coming mostly from other extremists.[4] It is extremely unfortunate when new technologies are used so as to increase the likelihood that members of deliberating enclaves will wall themselves off from opposing views.

But it is not difficult to imagine a very different kind of vision, one directly opposed to that offered by the Daily Me. Suppose, for example, that most people generally believe it important to seek out diverse opinions and to learn about an assortment of topics. Suppose, in other words, that the extraordinary opportunities provided by the Internet and other technological developments are regularly used as an instrument of citizenship—mostly national but sometimes even global citizenship, in which people continually enlarge their own horizons, often testing their own views by learning about alternatives. We could easily imagine a general social practice to this effect, even a cultural shift toward a society in which people became broadly committed to using the Internet in this way. To some extent, this shift is happening today.

We could also imagine a culture where aspirations of this kind were supported rather than undermined by private and public institutions. In such a culture, websites would frequently assist people in their desire to learn about other opin-

215

ions, even opinions different from those of the websites' creators. In such a culture, it would be common to provide links to sites with a wide range of views. And in such a culture, government would attempt, through minimally intrusive measures and perhaps only through moral suasion, to ensure that the system of communications was a help rather than a hindrance to democratic self-government.

Consumer and Citizen

Many people think that a system of communications should be evaluated by asking whether it respects individual choice. In this view, the only real threat to free speech is "censorship," conventionally understood. Speech is simply another commodity, to be chosen by consumers subject to the forces of supply and demand. With respect to ordinary consumer products, it seems natural to believe that the more people can "customize," or individuate, their preferred products, the better things will be. A well-functioning market for toasters, cars, chocolates, books, movies, and computers works better if it allows a large domain for individual choice—so that I will not have the same item that you have, unless this is what we want, in our individual capacities. For communications, as for cars and chocolates, one size does not fit all. Niche marketing is on the rise, and many people seem to think that the more niches, the better.

We have seen, however, that insofar as the Internet increases consumer choice, it is not an entirely unmixed blessing for consumers. The "consumption treadmill" means that for many products, people's purchases of more and better goods will make them spend more, and possibly much more, without really making them happier or improving their lives.

But the more fundamental problem is that a system of free expression should not be seen solely in terms of consumers and consumption at all. In a free republic, such a system is designed to maintain the conditions for democratic self-government—to serve citizens, not only consumers. Hence the public-forum doctrine ensures that the streets and parks are open to speakers, even if many of us, much of the time and before the fact, would prefer not to hear what our fellow citizens want to say.

When the public-forum doctrine was originally devised in the early twentieth century, avoiding streets and parks was far more difficult than it is today; hence the public-forum doctrine had immense practical importance. But this is decreasingly true. It is now entirely possible, and indeed increasingly possible, to spend little time in public forums. Largely by happenstance, general-interest intermediaries of the middle and late twentieth century—those who operate newspapers, magazines, and broadcasting stations—have done much of the historical work of traditional streets and parks. They promote exposure to issues and views that would otherwise escape attention, and that would not have been chosen before the fact. At the same time, they ensure a commonality of experience in a heterogeneous society.

In a free society, those who want to avoid general-interest intermediaries are certainly permitted to do so. No government agency compels adults to read or to watch. Big Brother is not watching you, and he is not watching what you watch. Nonetheless, a central democratic goal is to ensure at least a measure of social integration—not merely of religious and racial groups, but across multiple lines, in a way that broadens human sympathies and enriches human life. A democracy does not benefit from echo chambers or information cocoons. A society with general-interest intermediaries, like a society with a robust set of public forums, promotes a shared set of experiences at the same time that it exposes countless people to information and opinions that they would not have sought out in advance. These features of a well-functioning system of free expression might well be compromised when individuals personalize their own communications packages—at least if they personalize in a way that narrows their horizons.

I have emphasized throughout that a republic is not a direct democracy, and that a good democratic system contains institutions designed to ensure a measure of reflection and debate—not immediate responses to whatever people happen, at any particular moment in time, to say that they want. In this way, the original American Constitution was based on a commitment to a set of "filters" of a special kind—filters that would increase the likelihood of deliberation in government. The same commitment can be found in most democratic nations, which ensure against reflexive responses to popular pressures. Insofar as new technologies make it easier for people to register their short-term views and induce government to respond, they carry risks rather than promise. But insofar as new technologies make it easier for people to deliberate with one another, and to exchange reasons, they might carry forward some of the animating ideals of the system of free expression.

We have seen as well that it is unhelpful and implausible to say that with respect to the Internet and other communications technologies, "no regulation" is the path for the future. Any system that protects property rights requires an active governmental role, and that role takes the form of regulation, among other things allowing "owners," owing their status as such to law, to exclude people seeking access. If site owners and operators are going to be protected against "cyberterrorism" and other intrusions on their property rights, government and law (not to mention taxpayers) will play a central role. The question is not whether we shall have regulation, but what kind of regulation we shall have.

Free speech is never an absolute. Every democratic system regulates some forms of speech, not merely by creating property rights, but also by controlling a variety of forms of expression, such as perjury, bribery, threats, child pornography, and fraudulent commercial advertising (not to mention viruses sent by email). The question is not whether we will regulate speech, but how—and in particular how we can do so while promoting the values associated with a system of free expression, emphatically including democratic self-government.

I have also stressed the relationship between freedom of expression and many important social goals. When information is freely available, tyrannies are unlikely to be able to sustain themselves; it is for this reason that the Internet is a great engine of democratic self-government. Drawing on the work of economist Amartya Sen, and with particular reference to new technologies, I have also suggested that freedom of expression is central to social well-being, precisely because of the pressures that it places on governments. Recall Sen's finding that no society with a free press and open elections has ever experienced a famine. We should take this finding as a metaphor for the functions of freedom of expression in ensuring that governments serve the interest of their people, rather than the other way around.

Beyond Pessimism, Nostalgia, and Prediction

I have made three more particular suggestions. First, a communications system granting individuals an unlimited power to customize and to filter threatens to create excessive frag-

219

mentation. It would do this if different individuals and groups, defined in demographic, religious, political, or other terms, choose materials and viewpoints that fit with their own predilections while excluding topics and viewpoints that do not. This would undoubtedly produce a more balkanized society. The danger is greatly heightened by the phenomenon of group polarization, through which deliberating groups move toward a more extreme point in the same direction indicated by their predeliberation judgments. Indeed, the Internet creates a large risk of group polarization, simply because it makes it so easy for like-minded people to speak with one another—and ultimately to move toward extreme and sometimes even violent positions.

All too often, those most in need of hearing something other than echoes of their own voices are least likely to seek out alternative views. Often the result can be cybercascades of a highly undesirable sort, as false information spreads to thousands or even millions. We have seen evidence to this effect most vividly for extremist and racist organizations, but the point is far more general than that.

Second, a system of unlimited filtering could produce too little in the way of shared information and experiences. When many or most people are focusing on the same topic, at least some of the time, we benefit from a kind of social glue. The point is all the more important in light of the fact that information is a public good—a good whose benefits are likely to spread well beyond the particular person who receives it. General-interest intermediaries provide many advantages in this regard, simply because most of us obtain information that we then spread to others, and from which they benefit.

Third, a system of unlimited filtering might well compromise freedom, understood from the democratic point of view. For citizens in a republic, freedom requires exposure to a diverse set of topics and opinions. I have not suggested, and do not believe, that people should be forced to read and view materials that they abhor. But I do contend that a democratic polity, acting through democratic organs, tries to promote freedom, not simply by respecting consumer sovereignty, but by creating a system of communication that promotes exposure to a wide range of issues and views.

Nothing that I have said should be taken as an empirical argument about the likely choices of individuals in the next decades and more. Most of us have a great deal of curiosity, and we like to see materials that challenge us and that do not merely reinforce our existing tastes and judgments. This is demonstrated every day, not least by the truly astonishing growth of the number and diversity of sites on the Internet. I have emphasized that general-interest intermediaries continue to play a significant role, and that many of them are doing extremely well online. No one can know what the system of communications will look like in the long-term future. What I have attempted to do is not to suggest grounds for nostalgia or general pessimism, and much less to predict the future (in this context, an especially hopeless endeavor), but to explore the relationship between new technologies and the central commitments of a system of democratic self-government. Rather than being diverted by pessimism, nostalgia, and prediction, we should move beyond all three, in order to obtain a clearer understanding of our ideals and to see what might be done to realize them.

Franklin's Challenge

Recall Benjamin Franklin's answer to the large crowd asking the Constitution's authors what they had "given" to the American public: "A republic, if you can keep it." Franklin's answer was an expression of hope, but it was also a challenge, a reminder of a continuing obligation, even a dare. His suggestion was that any document committed to republican self-government depends for its effectiveness not on the decisions of the founders, and much less on worship of texts and authorities and ancestors, but instead on the actions and commitments of its citizenry over time. In drawing attention to the dangers posed by an "inert people," Justice Brandeis was merely carrying forward Franklin's theme.

My most general topic here has been the preconditions for maintaining a republic. We have seen that the essential factor is a well-functioning system of free expression—the "only effective guardian," in James Madison's words, "of every other right." To be sure, such a system depends on bans on official censorship of controversial ideas and opinions. But it depends on far more than that. It also depends on some kind of public domain in which a wide range of speakers have access to a diverse public—and also to particular institutions and practices, against which they seek to launch objections. It also demands not only a law of free expression, but also a culture of free expression, in which people are eager to listen to what their fellow citizens have to say. Perhaps above all, a republic, or at least a heterogeneous one, requires arenas in which citizens with varying experiences and prospects, and different views about what is good and right, are able to meet with one another, and to consult.

The Internet is hardly an enemy here. It holds out far more promise than risk. Indeed it holds out great promise from the republican point of view, especially insofar as it makes it so much easier for ordinary people to learn about countless topics, and to seek out endlessly diverse opinions. But to the extent that people are using the Internet to create echo chambers, and to wall themselves off from topics and opinions that they would prefer to avoid, they are creating serious dangers. And if we believe that a system of free expression calls for unrestricted choices by individual consumers, we will not even understand the dangers as such.

Whether such dangers will materialize will ultimately depend on the aspirations, for freedom and democracy alike, by whose light we evaluate our practices. What I have sought to establish here is that in a free republic, citizens aspire to a system that provides a wide range of experiences—with people, topics, and ideas—that they would not have specifically selected in advance.

ACKNOWLEDGMENTS

THE ORIGINAL edition of this book grew out of two lectures: the inaugural lecture for the Center on Law and Public Affairs at Princeton University and the closing keynote address for the symposium at Kent State University on the occasion of the thirtieth anniversary of the May 4, 1970 killings on that campus. I am most grateful to my exceptionally generous hosts on those occasions. At Princeton, particular thanks go to Stephen Macedo, Amy Gutmann, and Robert Willig for their hospitality, their comments, their skepticism, and their questions. Willig deserves particular thanks for critical comments that turned out to play a large role in the present edition. At Kent State, I am especially thankful to Thomas Hensley for his kindness and for helpful discussions. Faculty and students were extremely helpful on both occasions.

I am most grateful to my original editor, Thomas LeBien, for helping to give the book its basic direction, for general encouragement, and for superb suggestions. C. Edwin Baker, Mary Anne Case, David Estlund, Jack Goldsmith, Stephen Holmes, Lawrence Lessig, Martha Nussbaum, Eric Posner, Richard Posner, and David Strauss provided valuable suggestions and advice. Considerable help also came from four anonymous reviewers for Princeton University Press. Brooke May and Lesley Wexler gave superb and creative research assistance. Chapter 3 draws on my essay, "Deliberative Trouble? Why Groups Go To Extremes," *Yale LJ* 110 (2000), and I thank the *Yale Law Journal* for editorial help and for permission to reprint some sections of that essay here. Chapter 6 draws heavily on my discussion of blogs in *Infotopia: How Many Minds Produce Knowledge* (2006), though the discussion has been changed in many ways.

The idea for the current edition came from Chuck Myers, who also provided wonderful suggestions for how *Republic .com 2.0* should differ from *Republic.com*. I am grateful to Chuck for his enthusiasm and for strong encouragement to engage some of the excellent recent literature on the book's topic. I am also grateful to many people for valuable discussions since the publication of *Republic.com*, including Jack Balkin, Yochai Benkler, Larry Lessig, Douglas Lichtman, and Tim O'Reilly. Special thanks also to Spencer Short for superb research assistance and valuable comments.

NOTES

Chapter One: The Daily Me

1. See Nicholas Negroponte, *Being Digital* (New York: Knopf, 1995), 153. See also Robert Putnam, *Bowling Alone* (New York: Simon and Schuster, 2000), 177–79, for a prescient discussion of "cyberbalkanization," drawing in turn on an illuminating early paper, Marshall Van Alstyne and Erik Brynjolfsson, "Electronic Communities: Global Village or Cyberbalkans" (working paper, Massachusetts Institute of Technology, 1996), http://web.mit.edu/marshall/www/papers/CyberBalkans.pdf.

2. See Cass R. Sunstein, *Infotopia: How Many Minds Produce Knowledge* (New York: Oxford University Press, 2006).

3. The point is emphasized in Andrew Shapiro, *The Control Revolution* (New York: Public Affairs, 1999), from which I have learned a great deal, and many of whose concerns, including fragmentation and self-insulation, are the same as those stressed here.

4. See Yochai Benkler, *The Wealth of Networks* (New Haven, Conn.: Yale University Press, 2006).

5. See Sunstein, *Infotopia*.

6. For a valuable general discussion, see C. Edwin Baker, *Advertising and a Democratic Press* (Princeton, N.J.: Princeton University Press, 1997).

7. See Lawrence Lessig, *Code and Other Laws of Cyberspace* (New York: Basic Books, 2000).

8. See Lawrence Lessig, *Free Culture* (New York: Penguin, 2004); Benkler, *Wealth of Networks*.

9. On the Internet and equality, see Benkler, *Wealth of Networks*.

Chapter Two: An Analogy and an Ideal

1. Quoted in Alfred C. Sikes, *Fast Forward* (New York: William Morrow, 2000), 210.

2. In some ways these developments are entirely continuous with other important social changes. The automobile, for example, has been criticized for "its extreme unsociability," especially compared with the railway, "which tended to gather together . . . all activity that was in any way related to movements of freight or passengers into or out of the city" (George Kennan, *Around the Cragged Hill* [New York: W. W. Norton, 1993], 161, 160). Far more important in this regard has been what may well be the dominant technology of the twentieth century: television. In the words of political scientist Robert Putnam, the "single most important consequence of the television revolution has been to bring us home" (*Bowling Alone*, 221). And the result of the shift in the direction of home has been a dramatic reduction—perhaps as much as 40 percent—in activity spent on "collective activities, like attending public meetings or taking a leadership role in local organizations" (229).

3. Sikes, *Fast Forward*, 208 (quoting Alvin Toffler).

4. *Hague v. CIO*, 307 U.S. 496 (1939). For present purposes, it is not necessary to discuss the public-forum doctrine in detail. Interested readers might consult Geoffrey Stone et al., *The First Amendment* (New York: Aspen Publishers, 1999), 286–330.

5. See *International Society for Krishna Consciousness v. Lee*, 505 U.S. 672 (1992).

6. See *Denver Area Educational Telecommunications Consortium, Inc. v. FCC*, 518 U.S. 727, 803 (1996) (Kennedy, J., dissenting).

7. See the excellent discussion in Noah D. Zatz, "Sidewalks in Cyberspace: Making Space for Public Forums in the Electronic Environment," *Harv. J Law and Tech.* 12 (1998): 149.

8. See *Columbia Broadcasting System v. Democratic National Committee*, 412 U.S. 94 (1973).

9. An especially illuminating elaboration of republican ideals is Phillip Pettit, *Republicanism: A Theory of Freedom and Government* (New York: Oxford University Press, 1999).

10. See Gordon Wood, *The Radicalism of the American Revolution* (New York: Knopf, 1991).

11. From the standpoint of American history, the best discussion of deliberative democracy is William Bessette, *The Mild Voice of Reason* (Chicago: University of Chicago Press, 1984). There are many treatments of deliberative democracy as a political ideal. For varying perspectives, see Amy Gutmann and Dennis Thompson, *Democracy and Disagreement* (Cambridge, Mass.: Harvard University Press, 1998); Jurgen Habermas, *Between Facts and Norms* (Cambridge, Mass.: MIT Press, 1997); Jon Elster, ed., *Deliberative Democracy* (New York: Cambridge University Press, 1998).

12. To be sure, one of the central trends of the last century has been a decrease in the deliberative features of the constitutional design, in favor of an increase in popular control. As central examples, consider direct primary elections, initiatives and referenda, interest-group strategies designed to mobilize constituents, and public-opinion polling. To a greater or lesser extent, each of these has diminished the deliberative functions of representatives and increased accountability to public opinion at particular moments in time. Of course any evaluation of these changes would require a detailed discussion. But from the standpoint of the original constitutional settlement, as well as from the standpoint of democratic principles, reforms that make democracy less deliberative are at best a mixed blessing. Government by initiatives and referenda is especially troubling insofar as they threaten to create ill-considered law, produced by sound bites rather than reflective judgments by representatives, citizens, or anyone at all. For valuable discussion, see James Fishkin, *The Voice of the People* (New Haven, Conn.: Yale University Press, 1995).

13. H. Storing, ed., *The Complete Anti-federalist* (Chicago: University of Chicago Press, 1980), 2:369.

14. *The Federalist*, no. 81.

15. *Annals of Cong.*, 1st Cong., 1789, 733–45.

16. M. Meyers, ed., *The Mind of the Founder* (Hanover, NH: University Press of New England, 1981), 156–60.

17. Bill Gates, *The Road Ahead* (Rockland, Mass.: Wheeler, 1995), 167–68.

18. "The Emperor Strikes Back," *Entertainment Weekly*, January 7, 2000, http://www.ew.com/ew/report/0,6115,275009-2-3_7|| 260502|1_,00.html.

19. John Dewey, *The Problem and Its Problems* (1927; repr., Athens: Ohio University Press, 1980).

20. *Abrams v. United States*, 250 U.S. 616, 635 (Holmes, J., dissenting).

21. *Whitney v. California*, 274 U.S. 357, 372 (1927) (Brandeis, J., concurring).

22. For more detailed discussion, see Cass R. Sunstein and Edna Ullmann-Margalit, "Solidarity Goods," *J. Polit. Phil.* 9 (2001): 129.

Chapter Three: Polarization and Cybercascades

1. Putnam, *Bowling Alone*, 178.

2. See Robert Glenn Howard, "Sustainability and Narrative Plasticity in Online Apocalyptic Discourse after September 11, 2001," *J. of Media and Religion* 5 (2006): 25.

3. See Sikes, *Fast Forward*, 13–14.

4. See Shanto Iyengar and Richard Morin, "Red Media, Blue Media," *Washington Post*, May 3, 2006, http://www.washingtonpost.com.

5. Van Alstyne and Brynjolfsson, "Electronic Communities: Global Village or Cyberbalkans."

6. For a fascinating discussion, see Ronald Jacobs, *Race, Media, and the Crisis of Civil Society* (Cambridge: Cambridge University Press, 2000).

7. See Matthew Zook, "The Unorganized Militia Network: Conspiracies, Computers, and Community" *Berkeley Planning Journal* 1, no. 11 (1996): 26.

8. Ibid.

9. See Reid Hastie, David Schkade, and Cass R. Sunstein, "Political Deliberation and Ideological Amplification: An Experimental Investigation," *Cal L Rev* (forthcoming 2007).

10. See Roger Brown, *Social Psychology*, 2nd ed. (New York: Free Press, 1986), 222. These include the United States, Canada, India, Bangladesh, New Zealand, Germany, India, and France. See also, e.g., Johannes Zuber et al., "Choice Shift and Group Polarization," *J Personality and Social Psych.* 62 (1992): 50 (Germany); Dominic Abrams et al., "Knowing What To Think By Knowing Who You Are," *British J Soc. Psych.* 29 (1990): 97, 112 (New Zealand).

11. See D. G. Myers, "Discussion-Induced Attitude Polarization," *Human Relations* 28 (1975): 699.

12. Brown, *Social Psychology*, 224.

13. D. G. Myers and G. D. Bishop, "The Enhancement of Dominant Attitudes in Group Discussion," *J Personality and Soc. Psych.* 20 (1976): 286.

14. See ibid.

15. See Cass R. Sunstein et al., *Are Judges Political? An Empirical Analysis of the Federal Judiciary* (Washington, D.C.: Brookings Institution Press, 2006).

16. See Elisabeth Noell-Neumann, *Spiral of Silence* (Chicago: University of Chicago Press, 1984). See also Timur Kuran, *Private Truths, Public Lies* (Cambridge, Mass.: Harvard University Press, 1997).

17. See Robert Baron et al., "Social Corroboration and Opinion Extremity," *J. Exp. Social Psych.* 32 (1996): 537, 557–59n85 (showing that corroboration increases confidence and hence extremism).

18. Ibid., 541, 546–47, 557 (concluding that corroboration of one's views has effects on opinion extremity).

19. See Russell Spears, Martin Lee, and Stephen Lee, "De-Individuation and Group Polarization in Computer-Mediated Communication," *British J Soc Psych* 29 (1990): 121; Dominic Abrams et al., "Knowing What to Think by Knowing Who You Are, *British J Soc. Psych.* 29 (1990): 97, 112; Patricia Wallace, *The Psychology of the Internet* (Cambridge: Cambridge University Press, 1999), 73–76.

20. See John Turner et al., *Rediscovering the Social Group* (Oxford: Basil Blackwell, 1987), 142.

21. Spears, Martin, and Lee, "De-Individuation and Group Polarization."

22. See Wallace, *Psychology of the Internet.*

23. See R. Hightower and L. Sayeed, "The Impact of Computer-Mediated Communication Systems on Baised Group Discussion," *Computers in Human Behavior* 11 (1995): 2.

24. Wallace, *Psychology of the Internet,* 82.

25. For an overview, see Sunstein, *Infotopia.*

26. Thomas W. Hazlett and David W. Sosa, "Was the Fairness Doctrine a 'Chilling Effect'? Evidence from the Postderegulation Radio Market," *J. Legal Stud.* 26 (1997): 279 (offering an affirmative answer to the question in the title).

27. See Heather Gerken, "Second-Order Diversity," *Harv. L. Rev.* 118 (2005): 1101.

28. See Alan Kruger and Jitka Maleckova, "Education, Poverty, and Terrorism: Is There a Causal Connection?" *J Econ Persp* 17 (2003): 119.

29. Terrorism Research Center, "The Basics of Terrorism: Part 2; The Terrorists," http://www.geocities.com/CapitolHill/2468/bpart2 (quoting from "an essay from the US Army's Command & General Staff College in Fort Leavenworth, KS").

30. Ibid.

31. Jeffery Bartholet, "Method to the Madness," *Newsweek,* October 22, 2001.

32. Stephen Grey and Dipesh Gadher, "Inside Bin Laden's Academies of Terror," *Sunday Times* (London), October 7, 2001.

33. Margery Eagan, "It Could Be the Terrorist Next Door: Zealot Hides behind His Benign Face," *Boston Herald,* September 13, 2001, http://www.bostonherald.com.

34. See Russell Hardin, "The Crippled Epistemology of Extremism," in *Political Extremism and Rationality,* ed. Albert Breton et al. (Cambridge: Cambridge University Press, 2002), 3, 16.

35. See Caryn Christenson and Ann Abbott, "Team Medical Decision Making," in *Decision Making in Health Care,* ed. Gretchen Chapman and Frank Sonnenberg (Cambridge: Cambridge University Press, 2000), 267, 273–76.

36. Ibid., 274.

37. See Howard, "Sustainability and Narrative Plasticity."

38. See Sunstein et al., *Are Judges Political?*

39. See David Schkade et al., "Deliberating About Dollars: The Severity Shift," *Colum. L. Rev.* 100 (2000): 1139.

40. Diana Mutz, *Hearing the Other Side* (Cambridge: Cambridge University Press, 2006).

41. See ibid., 76–77.

42. Ibid., 85.

43. Ibid., 74–76.

44. Ibid., 75.

45. See, e.g., Sushil Bikhchandani et al., "Learning from the Behavior of Others," *J. Econ. Persp.*, Summer 1998, 151; Andrew Daughety and Jennifer Reinganum, "Stampede to Judgment," *Am. L. & Ec. Rev.* 1 (1999): 158.

46. See Timur Kuran and Cass R. Sunstein, "Availability Cascades and Risk Regulation," *Stan. L. Rev.* 51 (1998): 683.

47. David Hirshleifer, "The Blind Leading the Blind," in *The New Economics of Human Behavior*, ed. Mariano Tomassi and Kathryn Ierulli (Chicago: University of Chicago Press, 1999), 188, 204.

48. John F. Burnham, "Medical Practice à la Mode: How Medical Fashions Determine Medical Care," *New England Journal of Medicine* 317 (1987): 1220–21.

49. See Kuran, *Private Truths, Public Lies.*

50. See Matthew J. Salganik et al., "Experimental Study of Inequality and Unpredictability in an Artificial Cultural Market," *Science* 311 (2006): 854.

51. George Johnson, "Pierre, Is That a Masonic Flag on the Moon?" *New York Times*, November 24, 1996, sec. 2.

52. See Mark Granovetter, "Threshold Models of Collective Behavior," *Am. J. Sociology* 83 (1978): 1420; for a vivid popular treatment, see Malcolm Gladwell, *The Tipping Point* (Boston: Little, Brown, 2000).

53. See Lisa Anderson and Charles Holt, "Information Cascades in the Laboratory," *Am Econ Rev* 87 (1997): 847.

54. Several of these examples are discussed in ibid. and in Granovetter, "Threshold Models," 1422–24,

55. See Fishkin, *Voice of the People*.

56. Ibid., 206–7.

57. Ibid.

58. James Fishkin and Robert Luskin, "Bringing Deliberation to the Democratic Dialogue," in *The Poll with a Human Face*, ed. Maxwell McCombs and Amy Reynolds (Mahwah, N.J.: Lawrence Erlbaum Associates, 1999) 23.

59. See ibid., 22–23 (showing a jump, on a scale of 1 to 4, from 3.51 to 3.58 in intensity of commitment to reducing the deficit); a jump, on a scale of 1 to 3, from 2.71 to 2.85 in intensity of support for greater spending on education; showing a jump, on a scale of 1 to 3, from 1.95 to 2.16, in commitment to aiding American business interests abroad).

60. Ibid., 23. See p. 22 (showing an increase , on a scale of 1 to 3, from 1.40 to 1.59 in commitment to spending on foreign aid; also showing a decrease, on a scale of 1 to 3, from 2.38 to 2.27 in commitment to spending on social security).

61. For an early treatment see Bruce Murray, "Promoting Deliberative Public Discourse on the Web," in *A Communications Cornucopia: Markle Foundations Essays on Information Policy*, ed. Roger Noll and Monroe Price (Washington, D.C.: Brookings Institution Press, 1998), 243.

62. Sikes, *Fast Forward*, 15 (remarks of Paul Matteucci).

63. Jane Jacobs, *The Death and Life of Great American Cities* (1961; New York: Random House, 1993).

64. Ibid., 81, 95.

Chapter Four: Social Glue and Spreading Information

1. .See Amartya Sen, *Poverty and Famines* (New York: Oxford University Press, 1981).

2. See Amartya Sen, *Development As Freedom* (New York: Knopf, 1999).

3. Elihu Katz, "And Deliver Us from Segmentation," in Noll and Price, *Communications Cornucopia*, 99, 105.

4. See Putnam, *Bowling Alone*, 18–24.

5. See Chris Anderson, *The Long Tail* (New York: Hyperion, 2006).

6. Benkler, *Wealth of Networks*, 241–61.

7. Ibid., 242.

8. Ibid., 247.

9. Ibid., 253.

10. Ibid., 257.

11. See John Horrigan et al., "The Internet and Democratic Debate" (October 27, 2004), http://www.pewinternet.org/pdfs/PIP_Political_Info_Report.pdf

Chapter Five: Citizens

1. Robert H. Frank and Philip J. Cook, *The Winner-Take-All Society* (New York: Free Press, 1995), 201.

2. Alexis de Tocqueville, *Democracy in America* (New York: Knopf, 1987), 317.

3. John Dewey, "The Future of Liberalism," in *Dewey and His Critics*, ed. Sidney Morgenbesser (New York: Journal of Philosophy, 1977), 695, 697.

4. See Frank and Cook, *Winner-Take-All Society*, 19.

5. See Albert Hirschmann, *The Passions and the Interests* (Princeton, N.J.: Princeton University Press, 1967).

6. See Jon Elster, *Sour Grapes* (Cambridge: Cambridge University Press, 1983).

7. See Robert Frank, *Luxury Fever* (New York: Free Press, 1998) for a good discussion.

8. See ibid.

9. See ibid.

10. For a good overview, see Richard Layard, *Happiness* (New York: Penguin, 2005).

235

Chapter Six: Blogs

1. Jeffrey Henning. "The Blogging Iceberg," Perseus Development Corporation, 2003, http://www.perseus.com/blogsurvey/thebloggingiceberg.html.

2. Gary Becker and Richard Posner, "Introduction to the Becker-Posner Blog," http://www.becker-posner-blog.com/archives/2004/12/introduction_to_1.html.

3. Friedrich Hayek, "The Use of Knowledge in Society, *Am. Econ. Rev.* 35 (1945): 519, reprinted in *The Essence of Hayek*, ed. Chiaki Nishiyama and Kurt Leube (Stanford: Hoover, 1984), 211. A superb treatment of Hayek's thought is provided by Bruce Caldwell, *Hayek's Challenge: An Intellectual Biography of F.A. Hayek* (Chicago: University of Chicago Press, 2004).

4. Hayek, *Essence of Hayek*, 212.

5. Ibid., 214.

6. Ibid., 219–20.

7. Ibid., 220.

8. See Daniel Drezner and Henry Farrell, "The Power and Politics of Blogs" (2004), 12–13, http://www.danieldrezner.com/research/blogpaperfinal.pdf.

9. Aristotle, *Politics*, trans. E. Barker (London: Oxford University Press, 1972), 123.

10. John Rawls, *A Theory of Justice* (Cambridge, Mass.: Belknap Press, 1971), 358–59.

11. See Habermas, *Between Facts and Norms*, 940.

12. See Jürgen Habermas, *What is Universal Pragmatics?* in *Communication and the Evolution of Society*, trans. Thomas McCarthy (Boston: Beacon Press, 1979), 1, 2–4, 32 (discussing preconditions for communication).

13. Hugh Hewitt, *Blog: Understanding the Information Reformation That's Changing Your World* (Nashville: Thomas Nelson, 2005).

14. Ibid., 42.

15. Ibid., 36.

16. See Lada Adamic and Natalie Glance, "The Political Blogosphere and the 2004 Election: Divided They Blog" (2005), 4, http://www.blogpulse.com/papers/2005/AdamicGlanceBlog WWW .pdf.

17. Eszter Hargittai, Jason Gallo and Matt Kane, "Mapping the Political Blogosphere: Analysis of Large-Scale Online Political Discussion" (unpublished manuscript, Northwestern University, 2006).

Chapter Seven: What's Regulation? A Plea

1. John Perry Barlow, "A Declaration of the Independence of Cyberspace," http://homes.eff.org/~barlow/Declaration-Final.html.

2. If broadcast licenses were not allocated by the FCC, and if they were a more ordinary form of property right, exactly the same would be true! Property rights as we know them are created and protected by government. Of course this is not an argument against property rights.

3. See Richard Posner, *Catastrophe* (Oxford: Oxford University Press, 2003), 85.

4. See Friedrich Hayek, *The Road to Serfdom* (Chicago: University of Chicago Press, 1944), 38–39.

Chapter Eight: Freedom of Speech

1. For more detailed treatments, see Cass R. Sunstein, *Democracy and the Problem of Free Speech* (New York: Free Press, 1993): Alexander Meiklejohn, *Free Speech and its Relation to Self-Government* (New York: Harper, 1948); C. Edwin Baker, *Human Liberty and Freedom of Speech* (New York: Oxford University Press, 1995).

2. *Virginia State Bd. of Pharmacy v. Virginia Citizens Consumer Council*, 425 U.S. 748 (1976).

3. *44 Liquormart, Inc. v. Rhode Island*, 517 U.S. 484 (1996).

4. See *Buckley v. Valeo*, 424 U.S. 1 (1979).

5. See, e.g., *Randall v. Sorrell*, 126 S. Ct. 2479 (2006); *McConnell v. FEC*, 540 U.S. 93 (2003).

6. See, e.g., Thomas Krattenmaker and L. A. Powe, "Converging First Amendment Principles for Converging Communications Media," *Yale LJ* 104 (1995): 1719, 1725.

7. For discussion, see Lessig, *Free Culture*; Benkler, *Wealth of Networks*.

8. The old case, allowing government action, is *Red Lion Broadcasting v. FCC*, 395 U.S. 367 (1969).

9. See, e.g., *Denver Area Educational Telecommunications Consortium, Inc. v. FCC*, 518 U.S. 727 (1996). The Court's caution is defended in Cass R. Sunstein, *One Case at a Time* (Cambridge, Mass.: Harvard University Press, 1999).

10. See *Lochner v. New York*, 198 U.S. 45 (1905).

11. See Lessig, *Free Culture*; Benkler, *Wealth of Networks*.

12. For an effort in this direction, see Sunstein, *Democracy and the Problem of Free Speech*.

13. See ibid., 77–81, for an overview.

14. James Madison, "Report on the Virginia Resolution, January 1800," in *Writings of James Madison* vol. 6, ed. Gaillard Hunt (New York: Putnam, 1906), 385–401.

15. I draw here on Sunstein, *Democracy and the Problem of Free Speech*, 132–36.

16. *Pruneyard Shopping Center v. Robins*, 447 U.S. 74 (1980).

17. I attempt to answer it in Sunstein, *Democracy and the Problem of Free Speech*, 121–65.

18. The best discussion is Geoffrey Stone, "Content Regulation and the First Amendment," *Wm. & Mary L. Rev.* 25 (1983): 189.

19. See *Rumsfeld v. Forum for Academic and Institutional Rights*, 126 S. Ct. 1297 (2006).

20. The murkiness of current law is illustrated by the Court's decisions in ibid., in which the Court unanimously upheld the Solomon Amendment, withdrawing federal funding from educational

institutions that refused to provide equal access to the United States military; and in *National Endowment for the Arts v. Finley*, 524 U.S. 569 (1998), in which a sharply divided Court upheld a statute directing the NEA, when making funding decisions, to consider "general standards of decency and respect for the diverse beliefs and values of the American public." In the NEA case, the Court suggested that it would have ruled differently if the statute had discriminated on the basis of viewpoint.

Chapter Nine: Policies and Proposals

1. James T. Hamilton, *Regulation through Revelation: The Origin, Politics, and Impacts of the Toxic Release Inventory Program* (New York: Cambridge University Press, 2005).

2. A good discussion can be found in James Hamilton, *Channeling Violence* (Princeton, N.J.: Princeton University Press, 1998).

3. See Neil Gunningham and Peter Grabosky, *Smart Regulation: Designing Environmental Policy* (New York: Oxford University Press, 1999).

4. See David Messick and Ann E. Tenbrunsel, eds., *Codes of Conduct: Behavioral Research into Business Ethics* (New York: Russell Sage Foundation, 1997).

5. See Frank and Cook, *Winner-Take-All Society*.

6. *Red Lion Broadcasting Co. v. FCC*, 395 U.S. 367 (1969).

7. *Miami Herald Publishing Co. v. Tornillo*, 418 U.S. 241 (1974).

8. *Turner Broadcasting Co. v. FCC*, 520 U.S. 180, 227 (1997).

9. Ibid.

10. See Stephen Breyer, *Active Liberty* (New York: Knopf, 2005).

Chapter Ten: Republic.com

1. John Stuart Mill, *Principles of Political Economy*, 7th ed. (London: Longmans, Green and Company, 1909), bk. 3, chap. 17, parag. 14, http://www.econlib.org/library/Mill/mlP.html.

239

2. John Dewey, *The Public and its Problems* (New York: Henry Holt, 1927), 168.

3. See Gerken, "Second-Order Diversity."

4. See Hardin, "Crippled Epistemology of Extremism."

INDEX

ABC (American Broadcasting Company), 113, 154
abortion, 81
access rights, 204–6
African Americans: African American newspapers read by, 56; cascading belief regarding spread of AIDS among, 84–85; email rumor targeted at, 89
airports as public forums, 24
Alien and Sedition Acts, 178–79
al Qaeda, 75–76
Amazon.com, 20–21, 111
American Prospect, 159
Anderson, Chris, 110–11, 131
Anti-federalists, 35
Aristotle, 144
Arpanet, 157–58
Atrios, 138, 147
AT&T, 157–58
attention, commodity of, 206–10
Auletta, Ken, 19

Balkinization, 138, 146
Barlow, John Perry, 153
Benkler, Yochai, 114–15, 117
Berners-Lee, Tim, 158
best practices, 200, 202
Bill of Rights, 36, 38

Bin Ladin, Osama, 74
blogrolls, 209
blogs/blogosphere: anecdotal and empirical evidence regarding, 146–49; commodity of attention, proposal to leverage for public-interest goals, 209–10; deliberative democracy, as flawed contribution to, 144–46; growth of, 138; linking behavior in, 51, 115–16, 148–50; marketplace of ideas, as imperfect, 141–43; polarization, contribution to, 150; positive understandings of, 139
Bohnett, David, 49–50
Brandeis, Louis, xi, 41–43, 105, 179, 197, 205, 222
Brave New World (Huxley), xi
Breyer, Stephen, 205
British Broadcasting Network, 52
broadcasters, radio and television: disclosure policies, proposal for, 196–99; the fairness doctrine, 72–73, 198, 204–5; as general-interest intermediaries and public forums, 30–31 (*see also* general-interest intermediaries; public forums); government regulation of, argument opposing, 153;

241

248